Deacons, Wake Up!

A First-Century Call for Today's Servants

———— ❧ ————

J. J. Turner, Ph.D.

PUBLISHING DESIGNS, INC.

P.O. Box 3241 • Huntsville, Alabama 35810
256-533-4301 • www.publishingdesigns.com

Publishing Designs, Inc.
P.O. Box 3241
Huntsville, Alabama 35810

Printed in the United States

Library of Congress Cataloging-in-Publication Data

Turner, J. J.
Deacons, wake up! : a first-century call for servants in the twenty-first century to
imitate Jesus / J.J. Turner.
    p. cm.
 ISBN 978-0-929540-61-0 (alk. paper)
 1. Deacons. 2. Christian leadership—Biblical teaching. I. Title.
BV680.T85 2006
 253—dc22
                       2006032876
                       Rev.

Dedication

To the deacons of the McDonough Church of Christ:

Denny Dobbs

Kevin Holland

Danny Holtzer

Don Kirkpatrick

Ronny Maddox

Chris Martin

Jeff Wilder

Don Wilson

Todd Wilson

Contents

Ten Commandments for Deacons

Thou shalt meet the qualifications (1 Timothy 3:8–13).

Thou shalt do all to glorify God (Ephesians 3:21).

Thou shalt follow the Servant-King (Philippians 2:5–9).

Thou shalt not be afraid to get thy hands dirty.

Thou shalt serve with gladness of heart (Psalm 118:24).

Thou shalt do thy work with enthusiasm (Ecclesiastes 9:10).

Thou shalt be a team player (Ephesians 4:11–16).

Thou shalt serve out of love-motives (Mark 12:30–31).

Thou shalt prepare thyself for the work assigned.

Thou shalt be faithful in all things (Revelation 2:10).

Introduction

This book is the second in a series of wake-up calls for church leaders. In *Shepherds, Wake Up!* I made a plea for a return to the biblical emphasis on the qualifications and work of shepherds in the local church. This book is in that same vein: *Deacons, Wake Up!* is a plea to return to what the Bible teaches about the qualifications and work of deacons in the local church.

As we move deeper into the twenty-first century, the church faces staggering challenges both within and without. There are needs that didn't exist a few years ago. Likewise, ministries are being neglected and there is a shortage of servants. Fewer and fewer members want to be involved, which has given rise to increasing the paid staff to do the work. It used to be the "20–80 rule": 20 percent of the members do all the work and the 80 percent enjoy it. Now the rule is closer to 10–90.

It's time for deacons to take off their white gloves and go to work. It's time to pick up unused towels and do the work of slaves, just like the Servant-Savior did (Mark 10:45).

This book is an attempt to call attention to the need for training present deacons in the work of serving, as well as encouraging men to prepare themselves to become deacons in the local church. My prayer is that this material will be taught to the whole congregation, not to an isolated few. As congregations become better educated, the work of deacons will become more biblical, effective, and rewarding.

USING THIS BOOK

This book has been written to issue a wake-up call to all the men who serve as deacons, who aspire to serve as deacons, and for every member of the church, so that every member will be on the same page.

In order to gain maximum benefits from this book, I suggest you do the following:

1. Study it in a class situation.

2. Be sure each participant has a book.

3. Do extra research on each lesson, making it your "own."

4. Study each Scripture and how it relates to the lesson.

5. Use the "Thought and Discussion" section.

6. Work each "Case Study" in class.

7. Study the material thoroughly before coming to class.

8. Make up your own questions about the lesson.

9. Encourage personal application of the lesson.

10. Use the class time to discuss the major points.

11. Pray for wisdom.

12. Stay excited about the study.

1

A Wake-Up Call

LOSE THE SNOOZE

We have all checked into a motel and asked the desk clerk to give us a wake-up call to guarantee that we would get up early. On the other hand we have fallen into the trap of setting the alarm radio in the room, only to find ourselves playing tag with the snooze button. Oh, for just five more minutes—five more minutes—and five more minutes.

A wise-cracking speaker once said in a church after-dinner speech: "The elders are snoozing, the deacons have fallen asleep, and it is because the preacher is preaching Sominex sermons."

Wake-up calls are important in the issues of daily life. "The early bird gets the worm." We need a wake-up call in the church, especially among deacons. In too many congregations the snooze button has been set in concrete; deacons are asleep in the pilothouse while the old ship of Zion is headed for dangerous waters. It's time to wake up!

As we move toward the midnight hour that will usher in eternity, it is high time to "put on the whole armor of God" (Ephesians 6:11–18) and storm the stronghold of Satan (1 Peter 5:8). All of us, including the deacons, are soldiers of Christ fighting for the souls of men (2 Timothy 2:1–3; Mark 8:36–37). We need battle stations manned as never before. The brigade of servants must be on watch. Sound the alarm!

It's wake-up time! It's time for those men who serve in the special capacity of deacon to put their hands to the plow as never before. Every deacon in the church must wake up to some of the following truths, which in turn should ignite his fire so his service will be at a higher temperature.

→ It's Time to Wake Up . . . ←

◆ *Acknowledge that we are going in the wrong direction.* The church is declining in all areas: membership, attendance, giving, evangelism, mission work, leadership, and sound teaching.

◆ *Recommit to the eternal vision God has given the church (Isaiah 2:2–4).* This vision is the heartbeat of the church. Seeking and saving the lost must be our priority (Mark 16:15–16). Billions are walking toward eternity without the hope of eternal life (John 3:16; 10:10).

◆ *Close the back door through which new converts are leaving the church.* We must nurture and help these babes grow up in Christ (Ephesians 4:11–16; Hebrews 5:12–14). We must help keep the saved, saved.

◆ *Restore the spirit of boldness that existed in the first-century church (Acts 4:11–13).* We must not be bound by the spirit of fear (2 Timothy 1:7). We must not allow ourselves to fall into the trap of being "politically correct." Cowardice is condemned. Servants are brave!

◆ *Believe in the power of the gospel, the only message under heaven that can save sinful man (Romans 1:14–16; 1 Corinthians 15:1–4).* Fun and games won't save souls! Jesus saves (Matthew 1:21).

◆ *Get back to the preaching of the word of God with power, conviction, and enthusiasm (2 Timothy 4:1–6).* There is no place for wimpy preaching by soldiers of Christ. We're in a battle for souls!

◆ *Lift God up as the center of our worship (Isaiah 6:1–5).* We don't select what pleases our flesh but what pleases His heart. God is the one to whom we send our worship; we are the ones who offer it up "in spirit and truth" (John 4:24). What does God want?

◆ *Walk by faith and not by sight, knowing that without faith we cannot please God (Hebrews 11:6; 2 Corinthians 5:7).* Our faith must be larger than the balance on our check books.

◆ *Sacrifice time, talent, and money for the spreading of the gospel.* We need to have a selling-out attitude like our brethren had in the first century

(Acts 4:34–37). This is total commitment to the cause of Christ (Matthew 16:24).

◆ *Train and prepare men to serve in various leadership capacities in the church: elders, preachers, deacons, and teachers (Titus 1:5; 1 Timothy 3:1–7).* This will guarantee a sound and continuing future for the Lord's church (Acts 20:17–38).

◆ *Restore the moral purity of the church (Matthew 5:8).* The world must be left behind as we move onward in fulfilling the mission of the church (Philippians 2:4–9). Integrity and biblical values must be returned to the front burner of Christian living and service.

Are you awake? Do you get the message? It's time for a biblical wake-up call in the ranks of God's army, especially among the deacons. That's what this book is about!

LOOK IN THE MIRROR

Perhaps you are thinking, *I am only a server of tables; what do these things have to do with me?* They have to do with you because you are, or will be, a "special" servant in the Lord's church, and you must be concerned with these and other issues facing the church. You are part of the solution for two reasons: (1) you are a Christian and (2) you are a deacon (or will be). Every child of God must relate to these needs and issues in the church. But as part of the local leadership team, you have an extra measure of responsibility (Luke 12:47–48).

Integrity and biblical values must be returned to the front burner.

For some reason, deacons in the church have become a "laughingstock." Why? I'm not sure, but I suspect it is because many have fallen short of being what God demands. Second, it may be because many men are serving as deacons without proper training. And third, some aren't biblically qualified. Whatever the reason, it's time that the image of God's deacon takes on a new look. This new look begins with answering the wake-up call. Look in the mirror—what do you see?

It's wake-up time! Time for servant-soldiers of Christ to arise and take up a towel and serve in needed ways. There is no advantage in waiting until tomorrow. Each second we delay, a lost person dies somewhere in the world. There is a widow who needs food (James 1:27); there is a person who is down and out who needs help (Galatians 6:10). Needs are everywhere! There are tables that need bussing! Look around! There are ministry opportunities everywhere. Open your eyes!

Wake up and become a more dynamic servant!

My prayer is that this study about the deacon and his work will wake you up to a new awareness of how essential and important you are to the Lord's kingdom.

WHAT HAS HAPPENED TO GOD'S SERVANTS?

In a day when the church has a shortage of leaders in every category, and in a day when we have scores of in-name-only leaders, it's obvious that something has happened to God's servants. Men who have the title, men who have job assignments, men who should know what being a servant is all about have jumped ship. Many have gone on vacations or thrown up their hands in disgust.

Part of the wake-up call relates to the question: What has happened to God's servants? Where are they? Here are some possible metaphorical answers:

◆ They have gone to positive-thinking rallies.

◆ They have gone to cross-training classes to change careers.

◆ They have decided to do their own thing.

◆ They have moved into the corner office with a view.

◆ They have stepped on the neck of the competition.

◆ They have bought a getaway cottage.

◆ They have traded their towels for gadgets.

◆ They are fighting to stay on top.

◆ They have retired from service.

◆ They have changed their priorities and interest.

◆ They have quit because of discouragement.

◆ They are hiding in their comfort zones.

This book is prepared to help *you* wake up and become a more dynamic servant in God's mighty army. It's not a reflection on your present status, which may be at 101 percent, but rather a call to turn it up another notch. God wants each servant to be highly productive in the vineyard.

FOR THOUGHT AND DISCUSSION

1. Why may some deacons need a wake-up call?

   _____

2. What are some values of wake-up calls?

   _____

   _____

3. Is a wake-up call necessarily a negative thing?

   _____

4. What are some areas in which we need to wake up? Why?

   _____

   _____

   _____

5. How alert are you?

   ___sleeping ___snoozing ___slumbering ___awake ___wide awake

6. Why have some deacons become the object of ridicule?

   _____

   _____

7. What is your understanding of the word *servant* (deacon)?

   _____

8. Why is the morale low among some deacons?

9. What additional observations do you have?

10. How do you plan to use this lesson in your ministry?

→ CASE STUDY ←

The Downtown congregation was having problems with some of the deacons not fulfilling their ministry assignment. The question was: *How should this problem be approached?* It's easy to say, "We need a wake-up call." But we need something more than a wake-up call to get deacons to do their jobs properly. How would you sell the church on studying materials like those in this book? Be specific and biblical in your approach.

_____

_____

_____

_____

_____

_____

_____

_____

_____

_____

_____

_____

_____

_____

_____

_____

_____

_____

_____

_____

_____

_____

_____

CHAPTER

2

Unhappy Slaves

THE TWO-SIDED DEACON COIN

Several years ago I heard a speaker at a lectureship say that the elders are doing deacons' work, the deacons are sitting on the back pews with their coloring books feeling frustrated, and the preacher is running the church. I have reflected on those words numerous times over the years, wondering if they are true. Why do some churches have problems with deacons and some do not?

As I travel among congregations conducting leadership training programs, some of the most frequent remarks I hear relate to deacons and their work. There are two sides of the deacon coin. Here are some of the remarks I have heard, both positive and negative:

POSITIVE

◆ "Our deacons are on a roll . . . look out!"

◆ "We are blessed with great deacons."

◆ "If you want something done, give it to a deacon."

◆ "Our deacons are the greatest."

◆ "Our deacons are pace setters and dreamers."

◆ "We are losing a good deacon to the eldership."

◆ "Our deacons are very spiritual men."

◆ "Our deacons are Acts 6 deacons."

◆ "Our deacons keep us challenged."

◆ "Our deacons need to slow down."

◆ "I wish all our men were like our deacons."

Negative

◆ "How can we get our deacons to do their assignments?"

◆ "How do you train deacons to be servants?"

◆ "Our deacons are clueless."

◆ "We've got major problems with our deacons."

◆ "Some of our deacons think we [elders] should answer to them."

◆ "How do you remove non-working deacons?"

◆ "Our deacons need a shot in the arm."

◆ "Our deacons are deacons in name only."

◆ "Our deacons don't report or communicate in any way."

◆ "We've got deacons who don't have jobs. What should we do?"

The Local Setting

My experience tells me there are more negatives than positives relative to deacons and their work in some local congregations. This is why a wake-up call needs to be given across the brotherhood. Deacons, wake up!

Men serving as deacons under the Servant-Savior need to be reminded about the seriousness of their work. Playtime or coffee-and-donut-hour should not take up all their time. Their task is the lowly one of "washing feet"—getting down on their knees and doing what slaves do. Serve others, like the Master did (Philippians 2:4–9; Mark 10:45).

I would be amiss if I placed all deacons in the same category. The two lists above document how erroneous that would be. Each deacon must be judged individually, not in a category or group. I believe, as a whole, the men who have picked up the towel of servanthood want to do an effective job. Something, however, is preventing this from happening; but what? The purpose of this book is to provide some answers to this question.

The work of a deacon takes place within the local congregation, normally under the oversight of elders. It is in the local setting that his service takes place; and it is from this setting that he may reach out in ministry to the community (James 1:27; Galatians 6:10).

In order for deacons to function effectively and efficiently, they must be properly educated and trained for their ministries. This means that a proper environment must be created, an environment in which they are taught and helped to develop the skills essential to doing their work.

Deacons must be properly educated and trained.

Deacons are often assigned jobs they are not capable of doing effectively. Such assignments lead to low morale and frustration. I know of instances in which men were appointed as deacons with no ministries to perform. In some of those instances, the eldership believed if a certain man were made a deacon he would be more faithful in church attendance. That idea is not scriptural; it puts the cart before the horse. Faithful men are appointed to serve as deacons.

There is confusion and false teaching in some denominations relative to the selection, training, work, and authority of deacons. That same frustration and false teaching have made their way into the Lord's church. Add the influence of the secular models of leadership being used in the church and you have a major challenge: the challenge of educating the church on what the Bible reveals about the work of a deacon.

Let's take a few minutes and check your understanding of the deacon and his work:

⇥ CHECK POINT ⇤

1. How many studies have you had on the deacon and his work?

2. In your opinion what is usually neglected in the study of the deacon and his work?

3. What is the biggest challenge deacons face?

---

4. How important is it for the congregation to be educated in the work of deacons? Why?

5. Why are some qualified men reluctant to serve as deacons?

6. How have secular models of leadership impacted leadership in the church?

7. How often should a congregation study the work and qualifications of a deacon? Why?

8. How do most men learn how to be deacons? Why?

9. When does a congregation need deacons?

10. What determines the number of deacons a church needs?

BE PROACTIVE IN TRAINING

The church today faces challenges no other generation has faced. Many congregations are declining in number, scores are "holding their own," and sadly, many have ceased to exist. The challenges of evangelism, edification, and benevolence require that leaders take the lead. Elders must shepherd the flock, preachers must preach the whole counsel of God, and deacons must serve in the spirit of Christ (Philippians 2: 4–8).

Step up to the plate and serve— "as to the Lord."

This series of lessons is designed to sound a wake-up call for all deacons to develop the attitude of Christ, step up to the plate, and serve—to do the job assigned "as to the Lord" (Ephesians 6:7). Likewise, it is a wake-up call for elders and other church leaders to become proactive in training men to serve as deacons.

This book should be read and studied by every member of the church so all Christians can understand what the Bible teaches about the qualifications and work of a deacon. A prepared leadership team of elders, deacons, and preachers is a powerful force for doing God's work.

FOR THOUGHT AND DISCUSSION

1. What are your thoughts on the remarks about deacons and coloring books?

2. What negative remarks have you heard about deacons?

3. What positive remarks have you heard about deacons?

4. Why is it always appropriate to study what the Bible teaches about deacons?

5. What are some of the ways the work of a deacon is misunderstood?

6. How may we better prepare men to be deacons?

7. How has false teaching about deacons contributed to abuse and misunderstandings about their work?

8. Why does the entire church need education relative to the work of deacons?

9. What additional observations do you have about this lesson?

10. How do you plan to use this lesson in your ministry?

→ **CASE STUDY** ←

The Main Street congregation has a membership of five hundred, and is being served by seven elders, three preachers, and five deacons. The need for more deacons is obvious to the leadership, and several men are qualified. But some members believe the congregation has enough deacons. How would you respond to this situation? Be specific and biblical in your answer.

Who Wants to Be a Servant?

How to Be First

One day Jesus overheard His disciples arguing about who was going to be the greatest in the kingdom of God (Mark 9:33–34). These men were living under the iron fist of Rome and among the legalistic hands of the Pharisees. They had been waiting for God to send the deliverer. Now that the Messiah—the king of Israel—was here, the tables were about to be turned and they would soon be "bosses" or "rulers" in the new kingdom. They wanted power.

There seems to be in the base nature of man the desire to rule over others. The disciples were human; they wanted more than freedom. They wanted to be high in the pecking order; in fact, first place was the desired position.

The disciples were human; they wanted more than freedom.

Who would be honored with this position? Who would be the greatest? As they argued and debated the issue, the future king, who had come to be a servant, overheard them.

They didn't ask Jesus, but He knew what they were arguing about, so He responded, "If anyone desires to be first, he shall be last of all, and servant of all" (Mark 9:35). Wow! What an earth-shattering answer. Yes, you may be first, but in order to have that position you must go to the end of the line and find contentment in serving. That's God way.

Jesus didn't stop. He continued to clarify the road to being first.

> Then he took a little child and set him in the midst of them. And when he had taken him in His arms, He said to them, "Whoever receives one of these little children in My name receives Me; and whoever receives Me, receives not Me but Him who sent Me" (Mark 9:36–37).

Jesus didn't rebuke their desire for wanting to be the greatest. He simply responded with a positive lesson on how that greatness could be achieved. He taught them, using a child, that servanthood was innocent and freely given without prejudice. You become first by a willingness to be last. This is an attitude lesson that the Lord exemplified in His own life (Philippians 2:5–9), a tough lesson for today's deacons.

William Barclay made a relevant comment on Jesus' remarks about becoming like children:

> Now, a child has no influence at all. A child cannot advance a man's career, nor enhance a man's prestige. A child cannot give us things; it's the other way around. A child needs things. A child must have things done for him. And so Jesus is saying, "If a man welcomes the poor, ordinary people, the people who have no influence, and no wealth, and no power, the people who need things done for them, then he is welcoming me. And more than that, he's welcoming God." *The Gospel of Mark* (Philadelphia: Westminster Press, 1957), 231.

A New Leadership Style

A servant-leader must learn not to have respect of persons. He is on equal footing with all men. This being the case, how can he desire to be the greatest?

The Gospels contain additional accounts of the disciples' concern about who would be the greatest (Matthew 18:1–5; Luke 9:46–48; 22:24–27). Let's notice one of Luke's accounts:

> Now there was also a dispute among them, as to which of them should be considered the greatest. And He said to them, "The kings of the Gentiles exercise lordship over them, and those who exercise authority over them are called 'benefactors.' But not so among you; on the contrary, he who is greatest among you, let him be as the younger, and he who governs as he who serves. For who is greater, he who sits at the table, or he who serves? Is it not he who sits at the table? Yet I am among you as the One who serves" (Luke 22:24–27).

Jesus' works show a contrast between spiritual and secular leadership styles. He makes it clear that kingdom leadership will be the opposite of worldly leadership. Might will not make right. Old men won't arbitrarily rule. Jesus uses Himself as an example. He is a king by right of His divinity, but He chose to give up His equality with the Father to become a servant (Philippians 2:5–8).

I can imagine the thoughts that may have passed through the minds of the disciples when they heard Jesus' teachings on what would constitute greatness in the kingdom. His words were contrary to what they wanted or felt like they needed in order to topple Rome. They would never defeat their enemies with such a leadership style.

ROAD TO GREATNESS

If the call to servant-leadership was boat-rocking in the ears of the first disciples of Christ, it is of earthquake magnitude today. Really, who wants to be a servant? Today, even those who make excellent salaries as servants had rather be bosses. White collar, thirty-hour work weeks and stock options are what matter and signify that you are on the top rung of the ladder. Servant? No way! That's for the uneducated and unskilled.

In a power-hungry and position-struggling society, Jesus came as a "slave" to set men free (John 8:32, 36). He came to call and train a new breed of leadership— "foot washers" and "last in line" servants—leaders who didn't desire the head tables or the chief seats. This road to greatness in God's sight begins with a death to self and ego. Jesus said, "If anyone desires to come after Me, let him deny himself, and take up his cross, and follow Me" (Matthew 16:24).

> *Today, even well-paid servants had rather be bosses.*

Was Jesus out of His mind? How is it possible for a man to deny himself, take the last place in line, and become a great leader? *Servant*, as used by Jesus, described a special slave, a *doulos*. In that era, a *doulos* was on the bottom rung of the social ladder. A *doulos* was property and could be bought and sold at the owner's will. A *doulos* had no privileges or rights—no say-so, wants, or desires. His task in life was to do his master's bidding. Didn't Jesus know what the Exodus meant to the Jews? They would never be slaves again. This is why the disciples must have had difficulty in accepting Jesus' new style of leadership—servant-leadership, slavery!

In the first century several realities existed the life of a *doulos*.

1. He belonged to his master.

2. He owned no property.

3. He was often separated from his ancestors and immediate family.

4. He was stripped of his identity and dignity.

5. He was mistreated by unkind owners.

6. He was subject to unjust demands.

7. He could be sold with no choice in the matter.

8. He had no personal rights or options.

9. He worked without receiving the fruits of his labor.

10. He longed to be redeemed or set free from slavery.

SURRENDER TO SERVITUDE

To the early disciples it must have appeared that Jesus was asking them to trade one form of slavery for another. How could greatness come from giving up personal rights? How could a leader be great without having others serve him? In his book, *Celebration of Discipleship*, Richard Foster writes a wonderful observation about how giving up the right to be served sets you free:

> When we choose to be a servant, we give up the right to be in charge. There is great freedom in this. If we voluntarily choose to be taken advantage of, then we cannot be manipulated. When we choose to be a servant, we surrender the right to decide who and when we will serve. We become available and vulnerable. (N.Y.: HarperCollins, 1988), 132.

SO WHAT?

You may be asking yourself, *What in the world does this discussion about Jesus and slavery have to do with the work and qualifications of a deacon?* Everything! It sets the tone, as well as lays the foundation, for understanding the true nature of serving, which is what the work of a deacon is all about. In the words of Paul, "But now having been set free from sin, and having become slaves of God, you have your fruit to holiness, and the end, everlasting life" (Romans 6:22). We are free when slaves to Christ.

An understanding of Jesus' teaching on servanthood helps us answer the question, "Who wants to be a servant?" Every Christian, especially those who aspire to do the work of a deacon. Are you a servant? Do you want to be a slave?

The title of this chapter, "Who wants to be a servant?" could be somewhat misleading, especially in light of the fact that every Christian is identified by God as a slave (Romans 6:22). Being a servant is not optional. But serving in the special capacity as an appointed deacon who meets the qualifications outlined in the Bible is not required of every Christian, but only of those who are qualified.

Are you a servant? Do you want to be a slave?

It is from the general pool of congregational servants that special servants evolve. So first things first. If a man doesn't commit to function as a servant on the pew, it is doubtful that he will aspire to work as an appointed deacon. That is the reason it is essential for us to be reminded of the fundamental truth of the servanthood of every Christian.

❖ WHO WANTS TO BE A SERVANT ❖

1. Those who have denied themselves (Matthew 16:24).

2. Those who are following Jesus (John 13:12–17).

3. Those who are imitating Jesus (Philippians 2:5–9).

4. Those who have a "last of all" attitude.

5. Those who desire true greatness in the kingdom (Luke 22:24–27).

6. Those who want to do their duty (Luke 17:10).

7. Those who are called to be servants (1 Corinthians 7:21).

8. Those who acknowledge Jesus as Lord (Luke 6:46).

9. Those who are obedient servants (Ephesians 6:5; 1 Peter 2:18).

10. Those who serve the one Master (Luke 16:13).

11. Those who desire to serve others (Galatians 5:13).

12. Those who love Jesus (John 14:15; 15:14).

If you are a Christian, being a servant or minister of Christ is not a choice, that is, if you desire to please God. Before you aspire to do the work of a deacon, or work at your maximum effectiveness as a deacon, be sure your reasons for wanting to be a servant are the correct ones. Later when we study the selection of deacons in Acts 6:1–6, we will see that a unique spiritual background was required.

Who wants to be a servant?

FOR THOUGHT AND DISCUSSION

1. Why are persons interested in being the greatest?

2. Why were the disciples interested in knowing who would be first?

3. How did the Jews feel about being servants? Why?

4. Why did Jesus give up His equality with the Father?

5. Why did Jesus use a child to illustrate serving?

6. How does the average American view being a servant?

7. How may a person's ego stand in the way of serving?

8. Why is knowing the information presented in this lesson important to the work of a deacon?

   _____

   _____

9. What is a *doulos?*

   _____

10. How do you plan to use this lesson in your ministry?

   _____

→ CASE STUDY ←

The Central congregation had several works that were being neglected. It was proposed that several men be asked to serve as deacons. These men were appointed without any congregational, personal, or private study about the work of a servant in the church. How would you have suggested that the material in this lesson be used in helping the future deacons prepare for their assignments?

_____

_____

_____

_____

_____

_____

_____

_____

_____

_____

_____

_____

_____

_____

_____

_____

_____

_____

_____

_____

_____

_____

The Servant-King

JESUS BROKE THE MOLD

The supper had been congenial, even though it contained two sad realities: the Master's hour had come, and the devil had entered Judas' heart, urging him to betray Jesus. When the supper ended an amazing thing happened—a turning point in history occurred. Let's read that familiar account again:

> Jesus, knowing that the Father had given all things into His hands, and that He had come from God and was going to God, rose from supper and laid aside His garments, took a towel and girded Himself. After that, He poured water into a basin and began to wash the disciples' feet, and to wipe them with the towel with which He was girded (John 13:3–5).

A KING WASHING FEET! NEVER! NO WAY!

God on His knees washing human feet! Never!

Jesus broke the mold. The King of kings—God, who had come in man's nature—was on His knees washing the feet of lowly disciples. That humble act was so unthinkable that Peter dared to rebuke Jesus:

> "Lord, are You washing my feet?" Jesus answered and said to him, "What I am doing you do not understand now, but you will know after this." Peter said to Him, "You shall never wash my feet!" Jesus answered him, "If I do not wash you, you have no part with Me" (John 13:6–8).

No doubt Peter's intentions were noble, but he was way off target in his understanding of what Jesus was teaching. It was a message about true service, and who better to teach it than God in man's nature. Let's read the rest of the account:

You call me Teacher and Lord, and you say well, for so I am. If I then, your Lord and Teacher, have washed your feet, you also ought to wash one another's feet. For I have given you an example, that you should do as I have done to you. Most assuredly, I say to you, a servant is not greater than his master; nor is he who is sent greater than he who sent him. If you know these things, blessed are you if you do them (John 13:13–17).

SERVE ON YOUR KNEES

No greater model of servanthood can be found than the one exemplified by Jesus. For almost two thousand years it has inspired, encouraged, and motivated people to be servants. Former President Jimmy Carter wrote this about the influence Jesus' washing feet has had on his life:

> This kind of image [Jesus' washing the disciples' feet] is profoundly important to me as I try, in my own way, to follow Jesus' example: for instance, when I go with a Habitat team to build a house in Los Angeles or Chicago, inhabited by the poorest Americans, surrounded by drug addicts and criminals, sometimes with gunfire resounding on nearby streets . . . the awareness that my God walked this way before me makes it possible to sustain such an effort. *Living Faith* (N.Y. Times Books, 1996), 233.

There is no track of upward mobility in the ranks of kingdom servants.

Every Christian should apply to his life and ministry the lessons gained from the example of Jesus' washing feet. This is why it is especially an important model for deacons to imitate. There is no track of upward mobility in the ranks of kingdom servants. All serve equally on their knees with a towel. This is how their Master is served and pleased. There is no other way.

We've all heard the joke about the maid who wanted a job but made it known that she doesn't "do windows." In other words there were some tasks beneath her. This attitude is not limited to maids. Some servants in the church feel the same way. Jesus, however, conducted Himself in an opposite manner—no act of service was beneath Him; no person was outside His scope of caring. In His words: "For even the Son of Man did not come to be served, but to serve, and to give His life a ransom for many" (Mark 10:45).

Let's take a few minutes and survey some of the ways the Servant-King served and ministered to people:

→ How Did Jesus Serve? ←

◆ He washed feet, even the feet of His betrayer (John 13:1–17).

◆ He attended a wedding and helped (John 2:1–11).

◆ He socialized with outcasts (Luke 15:1–3).

◆ He fed the hungry (Matthew 15:32–39).

◆ He visited in the homes of those who needed Him (Mark 5:21–43).

◆ He associated with the outcast (John 4:5–26).

◆ He trusted people with assignments (Luke 10:2–12).

◆ He healed the sick (John 9:1–7).

◆ He comforted the bereaved (John 11:17–44).

◆ He taught many lessons (Matthew 5–7).

◆ He prayed for His followers (John 17:15–26).

◆ He chose unlikely men for leadership (Mark 1:16–20).

Jesus practiced what He taught. He lived in harmony with His claims of being a servant. He told His disciples, "For I have given you an example, that you should do as I have done to you" (John 13:15). Jesus wants deacons to serve others, regardless of their station in life. (He wants *all* Christians to don the attitude of service!)

You cannot serve as a deacon if you desire a seat at the head table, seek honored status, wear designer robes, or wait to be served. Jesus taught that you lead from the kneeling (humble) position. Slaves don't take themselves seriously; their recognition comes from their Master, who one day will say, "Well done, thou good and faithful servant" (KJV). This is the sought reward!

Jesus taught that you lead from your knees.

Deacons do not serve to please others but to please the one who has called them and given them a mission (1 Timothy 1:12). All actions come from the realization that it is a blessing and honor to follow in the steps of servanthood left by Jesus, the Servant-King.

THE SERVANT'S DUTY

Jesus not only demonstrated how a follower serves, but He also taught numerous lessons on how a follower serves. Note the account in Luke 17:7–10:

> And which of you, having a servant plowing or tending sheep, will say to him when he has come in from the field, "Come at once and sit down to eat"? But will he not rather say to him, "Prepare something for my supper, and gird yourself and serve me till I have eaten and drunk, and afterward you will eat and drink"? Does he thank that servant because he did the things that were commanded him? I think not. So likewise you, when you have done all those things which you are commanded, say, "We are unprofitable servants. We have done what was our duty to do."

The word *servant* is *doulos*. That means "slave." A master didn't give that kind of servant any special attention for serving well. Why? The servant was doing his duty; he wasn't due any special consideration, praise, or any other kind of acknowledgment. In fact, the master expected the servant to be a cook and a server of food. After he had served the master, he could eat.

After a slave had served the master, he could eat.

What a vital lesson for deacons! Deacons are assigned to do works for which they have volunteered. When the works are completed, no special recognition, reward, or honor is expected. They have just done their duty as servants in the body of Christ. The blessing of being able to serve is its own reward.

This doesn't mean that a church is forbidden to honor her deacons. Remember, it's the served, not the servants, who decide whether or not to reward those who serve. Servants have already been blessed by their acts of service.

In many congregations, special recognition of deacons is not a problem. In fact, it's just the opposite: they rarely receive any acknowledgment at all for the work they do. In my opinion this extreme is wrong, too.

VIEW FROM THE BOTTOM

In the secular world of leadership, the higher you climb the ladder of success, the more pressure you receive. This is why Jesus assigned His followers to the bottom rung—the last place in line. At the bottom of the pecking order:

there is no pressure.

there are no ego trips.

there is no competition.

there is no danger of losing your place.

there is no envy.

there is no faking it.

there is little danger of loss.

there are no usurpers.

there is no jockeying for positions.

there is no over-display of pride.

there is no expectation of special treatment or favor.

there is no self-serving agenda.

How ironic this sounds in our age of looking out for number one. But it's the way of the King who became a Servant in order to demonstrate what true servanthood in the kingdom was all about.

I have strong doubts that any man who does not understand the model of servanthood left by Jesus can serve effectively as a deacon. This is why this study must come before we jump into the work and qualifications of a deacon. Whatever the work and qualifications of a deacon are, they must be approached with the servant attitude of Christ (Philippians 2:5–8). He was the king who volunteered to become a slave! What will you volunteer to become?

FOR THOUGHT AND DISCUSSION

1. What was the occasion of Jesus' washing the disciples' feet?

2. Why did Peter respond negatively to Jesus?

3. How did Jesus break the mold? Why?

_____

_____

4. Why did Jesus choose to be a slave?

_____

5. To whom does Jesus' example of washing feet apply?

_____

6. Why don't we wash feet today?

_____

7. Discuss some ways Jesus served people.

_____

_____

8. How may a congregation become sidetracked in the mission of serving?

_____

_____

9. What may hinder a deacon from serving like Christ?

_____

10. Discuss the "servant's duty."

_____

_____

11. What is significant about the "view from the bottom"?

_____

12. How do you plan to use this lesson in your ministry?

_____

→ **CASE STUDY** ←

The deacons of the Downtown congregation were excited about the servant model of Jesus, so much so that they wanted to imitate what Jesus did by washing one another's feet, not as a binding commandment for today, but to get the feel of what happened. When this was made known in the church, there was a great controversy—some for and some against. If the deacons had asked you for advice, how would you have responded? Be specific and biblical in your answer.

It's about Serving

THE LOST MODEL

There are more models of Christianity than there are models of cars in America. Christianity as a whole is being presented to the world as a cafeteria: you may pass through the line and choose your favorite entrée. That idea raises a question: *What is Christianity all about?* Somewhere between the end of the first century and our present time, the model of the Servant-King has been lost. It has been replaced by the CEO and manager style of leadership—a leadership that is from the front, not from the knees.

Again, what is Christianity all about? If we answer that question based on the model of some of the twenty-first century churches, we may conclude there are several objectives of Christianity. Here are a few popular ones I have noted in our day.

→ POPULAR GOALS OF CHRISTIANITY ←

◆ To create and support a worshiping community.

◆ To develop and staff various programs.

◆ To foster long-held traditions.

◆ To equip and maintain physical facilities.

◆ To have an effective hired staff to minister.

◆ To conduct interesting Bible classes.

◆ To contend for sound doctrine.

- ◆ To develop a superior social environment.

- ◆ To take care of members.

- ◆ To entertain those who attend church services.

- ◆ To keep God trapped in our church buildings.

- ◆ To create a "segregated community" in the world.

- ◆ To change the political scene.

- ◆ To create a mega church to attract outsiders.

- ◆ To open for services four hours out of a 168-hour week.

CHRIST'S MISSION

What is your evaluation of what Jesus might think about His church being personified by some of these images? Personally, I believe the Servant-King would be displeased with many of the efforts organized in His name. Christ's name has been attached to everything from soup to salvation—a prostituting of His name.

> *The church of today must not only train servants but also practice serving.*

If Christ's mission emphasis was on serving, training servants, and teaching servanthood as conditions for kingdom-spreading, then it must follow that He wants His church to practice what He taught and commanded. He wants a galley of slaves rowing on the lower decks on the ship of Zion, while at the same time some are in the crow's nest searching for those who are perishing. Serving is a demanding job!

When compared to the span of time between Adam's sin and man's first offer of salvation by the gospel, Jesus' three-and-a-half-year ministry wasn't a very long time to set in place an eternal mission to redeem mankind (Ephesians 1:3–7). He had to select His priorities very carefully and focus on them.

Jesus didn't train an army; He didn't run for political office. He didn't organize protest marches, erect buildings, or cater to the rich and powerful. No, He chose to concentrate His ministry on the selection and training of servants, training them according to the model He demonstrated in His life. He trained kingdom-servants to train future kingdom-servants. So the church of today must not only train servants but also practice serving.

TEACH THEM TO OBSERVE COMMANDS

Christianity is about service. A church that isn't serving is not pleasing Christ. A church that is not equipping deacon-servants is not pleasing the Master.

Members of the body of Christ must be trained to minister to the body, as well as to the outside world (Ephesians 4:11–16; Galatians 6:10; James 1:27). The church is powerless if separated from her mission of service. Dr. Elton Trueblood writes these relevant words about the power of a few Christians centering their lives and ministry on the cause of Christ, as the twelve did in the first century:

> Christ's building of the little fellowship, on which depended the success of the entire enterprise, in both its endurance and its consequent penetration of the world, was the beginning of what we mean by the Church. If the faith is now forced to go on without it, the alteration in character will be so radical that what will remain will be a different reality altogether. What it may be, we naturally cannot know, but we can at least know that it will no longer be the Cause of Christ. *The Future of the Christian* (N.Y.: Harper & Row, 1971), 22.

The church is powerless if separated from her mission of service.

In order to understand properly the emphasis on serving Christ in and through His church, we must not forget the emphasis given in the *Great Commission*, not only teaching and baptizing, but also "teaching them to observe all things that I have commanded you" (Matthew 28:18–20).

The *Great Commission* requires the making of "learners" (disciples). This will include what Jesus taught about service and servanthood in the kingdom. As we have noticed in our previous lessons, Jesus taught, practiced, and trained a cadre of men to serve, who in turn were to teach others to serve, who in turn were to teach others to serve, thus passing the baton down to the twenty-first-century church (2 Timothy 2:1–3).

A Unique Breed

Words such as *servant, serve, service, minister, relief, ministration,* and *administer* in both the noun and verb forms are used more than ninety times in the New Testament. In every usage, regardless of the form, the emphasis is on service. But only five times in the English text do we find these words translated "deacon" and "deacons" (Philippians 1:1; 1 Timothy 3:8, 10, 12–13).

Very little is said about the official position of deacons in the church. There is only one clear example of their work, which is recorded in Acts 6:1–7, a passage we will study in detail. Servants stand apart from the crowd; they are a unique breed.

⇢ Identifying Marks of Bond-Servants ⇠

- ◆ They serve from a heart of love and compassion.

- ◆ They have a caring attitude that looks for needs to be met.

- ◆ They don't care who gets the credit; they just want to serve like their Master.

- ◆ They do what they do to be seen by the Lord, not for the praise of men.

- ◆ They understand that they are last in rank, feet-washers with no reputation or power.

- ◆ They know that Christ is seen in them as they go about doing good to all men (Galatians 6:10).

- ◆ They never brag or toot their own horns.

- ◆ They love the body of Christ and her mission in the world.

- ◆ They don't offer excuses to get out of "dirty work."

- ◆ They equate service with Christ-likeness.

It's about Serving

The Bible doesn't present the qualifications and work of a deacon as synonymous with that of a businessman or the manager of an organization. The organization of the local church is not a pyramid or hierarchical structure styled after the world. In contrast, Jesus created a horizontal structure, where there is one head, Him, with everyone else on the same level or rank, serving under the head. There is not a big "I" and little "you," so understanding the importance of each member, as well as his function in the body, is very important to serving effectively as a deacon in the local church (1 Corinthians 12:12–27).

The deacon is under the authority of Christ and the Scripture, not under the authority of men. His position enables him to minister to others who are on his level but who are not yet qualified to serve as deacons.

The Bible does not present an example of a "Board of Deacons" that is appointed to direct the affairs of the church. There is no example of deacons doing anything other than serving the needs of others. There is not an example of deacons occupying a perpetual office. There was a special work (ministry) that needed to be done, and special men were appointed to do it. These men were deacons, not bosses or under-shepherds. They were slaves who had dedicated themselves to serving their Master.

The Bible does not present an example of a "Board of Deacons."

The work of a deacon is about serving!

For Thought and Discussion

1. Why is there confusion about the nature of Christianity?

2. Why are there so many models of Christianity?

3. What are some additional misconceptions of Christianity?

4. What do you imagine Jesus thinks about the ways His church is personified today?

5. How does servanthood relate to spreading the kingdom?

   _____

6. How did Jesus use His time to train servants?

   _____

7. Why must a deacon understand that the nature of Christianity is service?

   _____

8. How does the mission of the church affect how a deacon serves?

   _____

9. How does the *Great Commission* relate to a deacon's work?

   _____

10. Why are deacons a "unique breed"?

    _____

11. How do you plan to use this lesson in your ministry?

    _____

─── ✢ **Case Study** ✢ ───

The deacons of the Valley church meet each month to discuss various works of the church and how they should be accomplished. In a recent meeting a new deacon objected to what he called a too-business approach to their work. How would you respond to this issue if asked to help? Be specific and biblical in your answers.

6

A Call for Slaves

1796 Newspaper: Want Ad

Wanted for a sober family, a man of light weight, who fears the Lord and can drive a pair of horses. He must occasionally wait at table, join in a household prayer, look after horses and read a chapter in the Bible. He must, God willing, rise at seven in the morning, and obey his master and mistress in all lawful commands; if he can dress hair, sing psalms and play cribbage, the more agreeable. He must not be familiar with the maid servants, lest the flesh should rebel against the spirit and he should be induced to walk in the thorny paths of the wicked. Wages 15 guineas a year [about $7 a month].

I wonder how many men responded to that ad. Perhaps in its day it was the norm, but in our day it smacks at unreasonableness and slavery. Call the Labor Department or a labor union to get an official statement on the ad's legality.

Dedicated men who are willing to serve are rare. The Marines are looking for "a few good men." "A good man is hard to find" is more than a line in a song. In the unfaithful times in Israel, God "sought for a man . . . and found no one"! (Ezekiel 22:30).

When Jesus issued the "follow me" command and the promise to make those who followed fishers of men (Mark 1:16–17), He was inviting them to a walk in servanthood, a path He would create and leave for them.

WHERE GOD FOUND SERVANTS

When God needed servants He did not go to the employment agencies and contract for temporary help. Neither did He run ads in the paper nor pass His needs around by word of mouth.

⇢ GOD'S SERVANTS ⇠

- *Noah* was actively involved in the daily affairs of life when God called him to build the ark (Genesis 6:8–7:6).

- *Abraham* was enjoying his family and homeland when God called him to go to parts unknown (Genesis 12:1–5).

- *Moses* was on the back side of a mountain living a quiet and peaceful life when God called him into service (Exodus 3:1–4:22).

- *David* was herding sheep when he was called into service against the Philistines (1 Samuel 17: 33–58).

- *Esther* was in bondage when she was called to serve God in the king's palace (Esther 2:5–12; 4:14).

- *Job* was called from his riches to be God's suffering servant (Job 2:1–13).

- *Amos* was called from being a dresser of trees to become a prophet (Amos 7:14–17).

- *John the Baptist* was called from the wilderness to die for truth (Matthew 3:1–17).

- *The disciples* were called from fishing boats and tax tables to search for the lost (Mark 1:16–20; Matthew 9:9).

- *Paul* was called from persecuting Christians to a life of defending Christianity's founder (Acts 9:1–20).

The call to servanthood does not depend on geography or outward trappings; rather, it is based on what's in the servant's heart. "Man looks at the outward appearance, but the Lord looks at the heart" (1 Samuel 16:7).

God is still calling servant-leaders by the gospel (2 Thessalonians 2:13–14). He is searching hearts for a few good men. Are you one of these men? Are you a servant?

WHERE YOU WILL NOT USUALLY FIND SERVANTS

Just as men look for love in all the wrong places, we sometimes look in all the wrong places for servants. There are a number of places you will not usually find servants in the biblical usage of the word *doulos:*

1. You will not usually find servants in the President's suite.

2. You will not usually find servants in *Who's Who* listings.

3. You will not usually find servants in the "winner's circles."

4. You will not usually find servants in a bragging contest.

5. You will not usually find servants seated at the head of the table.

6. You will not usually see servants on the *Lifestyles of the Rich and Famous* TV program.

7. You will not usually find servants in the ruts of resentments.

8. You will not usually find servants in power-ploy meetings.

9. You will not usually find servants pushing "little people" around.

10. You will not usually find servants in the ranks of the unhappy.

I am not saying that all these areas are wrong or sinful. I am saying that in these areas you will not usually find the quality of character God desires in servants who are striving to be Christ-like.

POOR IN SPIRIT

In His great transitional sermon, the *Sermon on the Mount*, Jesus set forth the route to true servanthood and acceptance by God:

> Blessed are the poor in spirit, for theirs is the kingdom of heaven. Blessed are those who mourn, for they shall be comforted. Blessed are the meek, for they shall inherit the earth. Blessed are those who hunger and thirst for righteousness, for they shall be filled. Blessed are the merciful, for they shall obtain mercy. Blessed are the pure in heart, for they shall see God. Blessed are the peacemakers, for they shall be called sons of God (Matthew 5:3–9).

Yes, these "be-attitude" qualities are essential for every person who desires to follow Jesus, but they are especially applicable to those who aspire to serve as deacons in the Lord's church. Every venture begins somewhere, and servanthood begins with being poor in spirit. It is an attitude that says I have nothing to boast about. I can't save myself or even direct my footsteps. I need a Savior. It's an attitude that cries out for help.

HOW THE CALL TO SERVANTHOOD COMES

There is nothing mysterious or rare about the way God calls men to serve as deacons. The call to servanthood doesn't come in a still, small voice in the middle of the night. Neither does an angel come and tap a chosen deacon on the shoulder and say it's time. A number of things are involved in a man's becoming a deacon in the church, or as we might say, the way a man is called to serve. Here are some of those dynamics:

1. He has first answered the gospel call to salvation (2 Thessalonians 2:13–14). It takes a saved man to serve the King of kings as the King desires.

2. He is a man who understands, believes in, and wants to participate in the mission of the church on earth (Matthew 28:18–20).

3. He is a man who has the great commandment on straight. He loves as he should (Mark 12:28–34).

4. He is a Christian who has a heart full of compassion and is willing to serve out of a sense of truly caring (Philippians 2:20).

5. He is a dedicated, faithful member of a local congregation (Hebrews 10:24–25; 6:1–6).

6. He is a wise and spiritual man who has developed skills and knowledge that qualify him to serve as a deacon.

7. He is a man who has the attitude of Christ, which is the attitude of gladly becoming a slave-servant (Philippians 2:5–8).

8. He is zealous for good works (Titus 2:14).

There is no biblical evidence that God has ever called a lazy person or an inactive person to the forefront of kingdom-service. God uses men who have proved their commitment and faithfulness. Jesus uses men who have signed up for the duration. He taught: "No one, having put his hand to the plow, and looking back, is fit for the kingdom of God" (Luke 9:62).

FOR THOUGHT AND DISCUSSION

1. Discuss the 1796 newspaper ad.

2. Why do most organizations look for dedicated people?

3. How did God find and call His servants?

4. How does the call of God's servants recorded in the Bible relate to servants in the church?

5. Why is the heart so important in being a servant?

6. List some additional places you will not find God's servants.

7. How does the *Sermon on the Mount* relate to being a servant in the church?

8. Discuss how the call to servanthood comes today.

9. How does God use lazy people?

10. What additional observations do you have?

11. How do you plan to use this lesson in your ministry?

→ **CASE STUDY** ←

The elders of the River Street church posted a list of congregational works on the bulletin board, asking for volunteers to sign up for the work of their choice. Those who signed up would be designated deacons. As a member of the congregation, knowing what you do about the work and qualifications of deacons, how would you approach the elders about their decision? Be specific and biblical in your answer.

Attributes of
Servant-Leaders

QUALITIES VERSUS QUALIFICATIONS

How God evaluates a servant is more important than how man evaluates him. In the book of Job, God asked Satan:

> "From where do you come?" So Satan answered the Lord and said, "From going to and fro on the earth, and from walking back and forth on it." Then the Lord said to Satan, "Have you considered My servant Job, that there is none like him on the earth, a blameless and upright man, one who fears God and shuns evil? And still he holds fast to his integrity" (Job 2:2–3).

I am in awe when I consider what God said about His servant Job: "There is none like him." This lets us know that God is aware of who and what His servants are. All God's servants, whether general Christian-servants or special deacon-servants, must possess certain positive attributes that please God.

We must not think that a deacon has to meet only the few qualifications outlined in the New Testament, and then he is ready to serve. There are attributes that go much deeper than qualifications. There are numerous qualities that a deacon-leader must possess in order to be an effective servant. Study carefully and prayerfully the following general attributes. They are based on biblical principles and deal with some of the core qualities a man needs before he is appointed to serve tables. As you study these attributes ask yourself these questions:

◆ What does this attribute really mean to my life and ministry?

◆ How proficient am I in demonstrating this attribute in my work as a deacon (or other leadership role)?

◆ What do I need to do in order to develop this servant-quality in my life?

◆ How can I use this attribute in my work as a deacon (or other servant-leader)?

◆ How can I help others develop these qualities in their lives?

These points are brief, so be sure to take time to reflect on each one so you will gain the maximum benefits:

1. *No deacon can serve two masters*: "No one can serve two masters; for either he will hate the one and love the other, or else he will be loyal to the one and despise the other. You cannot serve God and mammon" (Matthew 6:24). God will not ride in the back-seat or occupy second place in your life. He must be first and you must be His servant, first and foremost (Matthew 6:33).

2. *Deacons must serve the Lord whole-heartedly*, "With goodwill doing service, as to the Lord, and not to men, knowing that whatever good anyone does, he will receive the same from the Lord, whether he is a slave or free" (Ephesians 6:7–8). This simply means, give your all in God's service.

3. *Deacons do not serve programs or self.* They serve the one true and living God: "How much more shall the blood of Christ, who through the eternal Spirit offered Himself without spot to God, cleanse your conscience from dead works to serve the living God?" (Hebrews 9:14; cf. Revelation 5:10). Through serving God, deacons serve people.

4. *Jesus' servants are promised a place with Him, which is a great incentive for serving*: "If anyone serves Me, let him follow Me; and where I am, there My servant will be also. If anyone serves Me, him My Father will honor" (John 12:26).

5. *God's servant must not be a troublemaker, but a person of peace:* "And a servant of the Lord must not quarrel but be gentle to all, able to teach, patient" (2 Timothy 2:24). Did you notice that a servant must be kind to everyone? How do you do this in your life and ministry?

6. *Servants who serve faithfully will one day hear these words:* "Well done, good and faithful servant" (Matthew 25:21). Can you imagine hearing these words? This promise makes the trials of servanthood worthwhile.

7. *Servant-leaders must serve the Lord enthusiastically from the heart:* "Not lagging in diligence, fervent in spirit, serving the Lord" (Romans 12:11). This is an infectious quality in the life of a service-driven deacon in the church.

8. *Servants are faithful in their service to the Lord and the church unto death;* there are no retirement plans. Jesus said, "Be faithful until death [even to the point of death], and I will give you the crown of life" (Revelation 2:10). This quality was exemplified in the life of Paul (2 Timothy 4:6–8).

9. *Servants model divine love among their followers:* "By this all will know that you are My disciples, if you have love for one another" (John 13:35). Love is a badge of the people-driven deacon.

10. *Servants don't try to out guess God or run ahead of Him:* "Instead you ought to say, 'If the Lord wills, we shall live and do this or that.' But now you boast in your arrogance. All such boasting is evil" (James 4:15–16).

11. *Servants don't try to serve by proxy.* They know no one else can fulfill their ministry for them. They must do it themselves. This is not a rebuke against delegation, but an observation about personal responsibility as a deacon.

12. *Servants don't try to put new wine into old wine skins.* They know the church is in the twenty-first century, not the nineteenth or

eighteenth. Change doesn't scare them so long as it is in harmony with the word of God. They know the difference between expediencies and the bound commands in the Bible.

NONE LIKE HIM

The church is being led and served by various models of servants, from the CEO model to the haphazard model. Some churches are micromanaged; others are left to the "drifting model." Many congregations are stalled at status quo. Some are dying, some are waiting to have the closing prayer announcing their end, and a few are growing as a result of reaching the lost outside their buildings.

Every congregation that has deacons should expect these servants to possess spiritual qualities that feed into their ministries. It is out of *what* they *are* that what they *do* evolves.

May each deacon in the Lord's church have as his goal the words that God said about Job: "There is none like him on the earth." By prayerfully and diligently applying Job's qualities to his life, a deacon will be moving in the direction of hearing God pronounce these words about him.

FOR THOUGHT AND DISCUSSION

1. Why did God choose Job as His test case for faithfulness?

   _____

2. How does the story of Job apply to the work of a deacon?

   _____

3. Why must a deacon first *be* something before he can *do* something?

   _____

4. How does character relate to the work of a deacon?

   _____

5. Discuss some of the main points in this lesson.

   _____

   _____

6. What challenged you most in this lesson? Why?

_____

_____

7. How may this lesson make a difference in your service as a deacon or some other Christian worker?

_____

8. When should an aspiring deacon know these truths? Before or after he is appointed as a deacon?

_____

9. What additional observations do you have?

_____

10. How do you plan to use this lesson in your ministry?

_____

→ **CASE STUDY** ←

The church knew it was time to study the work and qualifications of deacons. The Uptown congregation needed several men to serve in new ministries. While discussing the agenda for the study, it was suggested that the first part of the study focus on the character and spiritual qualities of men who could serve. After that, their qualifications should be compared to the guidelines for deacons as set forth in the Bible. Some objected to that approach and suggested that they needed to get right into the qualifications. How would you have responded to this attitude? Be specific and biblical in your answer.

_____

_____

_____

_____

_____

_____

_____

_____

_____

_____

_____

_____

_____

_____

_____

_____

_____

_____

_____

_____

Slaves' Hall of Fame

DEEDS ENSHRINED

America is famous for its numerous halls of fame, places of honor set aside to enshrine the deeds of a few chosen people from sports, music, entertainment, and such like. In Hebrews 11 we have "The Hall of the Faithful," God's list of outstanding characters who have honored Him by deeds of faith. What an inspiration to faithful service!

Tucked away in the pages of the New Testament are the names and accounts of various slaves (servants), who, in my opinion, are members of the "Slaves' Hall of Fame." But the most outstanding example is found in Luke 10.

A NAMELESS SLAVE CALLED "GOOD"

Next to the account of Jesus' washing the disciples' feet, the story of the "Good Samaritan" is probably the most famous account of service in the New Testament. Let's notice the account of a man who is nameless, but for obvious reasons he has been given the name "Good."

And behold, a certain lawyer stood up and tested Him, saying, "Teacher, what shall I do to inherit eternal life?" He said to him, "What is written in the law? What is your reading of it?" So he answered and said, "'You shall love the Lord your God with all your heart, with all your soul, with all your strength, and with all your mind,' and 'your neighbor as yourself.'" And He said to him, "You have answered rightly; do this and you will live." But he, wanting to justify himself, said to Jesus, "And who is my neighbor?" Then Jesus answered and said: "A certain man went down from Jerusalem to Jericho, and fell among thieves, who stripped him of his clothing, wounded him, and departed, leaving him half dead. Now by chance a certain priest came down that road. And when he saw him, he passed by on the other side. Likewise a Levite, when he arrived at the place, came and looked, and passed by on the other side. But a certain Samaritan, as he journeyed, came where he was. And when he saw him, he had compassion. So he went to him and bandaged his wounds, pouring on oil and wine; and he set him on his own animal, brought him to an inn, and took care of him. On the next day, when he departed, he took out two denarii, gave them to the innkeeper, and said to him, 'Take care of him; and whatever more you spend, when I come again, I will repay you.' So which of these three do you think was neighbor to him who fell among the thieves?" And he said, "He who showed mercy on him." Then Jesus said to him, "Go and do likewise" (Luke 10:25–37).

I am always amazed and challenged by this parable taught by the Chief Servant, Jesus. It contains numerous lessons relevant to the work of service in the church and is a model of attitude for all who desire to please the Lord as deacons.

Evolving out of a question relating to eternal life came some amazing truths about who is a true neighbor. It was not the pious priest and religious Levite coming from their duties in the temple. How ironic for men to have been on their way from "church" where they had served, praised, and honored God but had no time to practice what God really wanted: caring for those in need. They had their creed right but their hearts were wrong! Jesus, as He so frequently did, upset the apple cart by introducing an unnamed man called a "certain Samaritan." This would have been an automatic turn-off to the lawyer, but he had asked the question and must hear the answer.

There are numerous truths related to serving found in this great parable:

→ TRUTHS FROM THE SAMARITAN ←

- People within our awareness have been stripped, wounded, and robbed.

- Religiosity or piousness alone doesn't minister to the needy.

- Seeing, looking closely, and mouthing platitudes don't meet the needs of hurting people (James 2:14–26).

- Help must not be postponed. The Samaritan did what he could immediately, where he found the victim. He didn't take time to "check the wounded man out" or call a business meeting to see if he should help. He responded immediately out of a caring heart.

- The Samaritan placed his own safety in jeopardy. This might have been a waylay trap set by robbers to lure another victim. He wasn't afraid. The need was greater than any fear he might have had.

- He was a hands-on helper. He saw a need and responded to it without thinking twice. He must have had a habit of caring and made an automatic response.

- He relinquished his own comfort by walking while the injured man rode his animal. Caring goes the second mile.

- He took the wounded man to a place where he could be helped, and stayed the night.

- He took money from his own pocket to pay for services rendered. He assured the innkeeper, who perhaps knew him, that when he returned he would pay all additional expenses. He was interested in the long-range care of the victim, not just the immediate needs.

- The Samaritan, who is nameless in the parable, has been given the name "Good." Why? Because he did good.

DO LIKEWISE

The lawyer was backed into a corner when Jesus asked him, "So which of these three do you think was neighbor to him who fell among the thieves?" (Luke 10:36). He honestly uttered the correct answer: "He who showed mercy on him." Then the next shoe dropped: Jesus said, "Go and do likewise" (Luke 10:37). Go and do what? Go and help someone in need; that's how you demonstrate your love for God and your neighbor. That's how you serve God.

You might be thinking, *What does this have to do with serving as a deacon in the local church?* It is one of the many lessons Jesus taught on the true nature of servant-hood. The qualities seen in the service rendered by the good Samaritan are what Jesus requires of all His under-servants, but especially of deacons who have stepped forward to take on the special ministries of serving. It

The need was greater than any fear he might have had.

settles once and for all the questions about to whom should we minister: Anyone who needs help! (See Galatians 6:10; James 1:27.)

ROLL CALL OF SERVANTS

While the story of the "Good Samaritan" is the most extensive account exemplifying what it means to meet the needs of a person through true service, there are many other persons identified in the New Testament as servants. The very fact they are called servants in various texts by the Holy Spirit tells us volumes about them. As we walk through the "Slaves' Hall of Fame" let's notice other names:

- Epaphras (Colossians 1:7).
- Epaphroditus (Philippians 2:25, 30).
- Tychicus (Colossians 4:7).
- Onesimus (Philemon 10–11, 13).
- Mark (2 Timothy 4:11).
- Paul (2 Corinthians 11:7–8).
- Timothy and Erastus (Acts 19:22).
- Phoebe (Romans 16:1–2).
- Mary (Romans 16:6).
- Stephanas (1 Corinthians 16:15–16).
- Barnabas (Acts 4:36–37).

When a twenty-first-century deacon picks up his towel to serve, he is joining an elite rank of slaves. What an honor to be identified with such a group; especially with the Chief Servant Himself, Jesus Christ.

The road to servanthood begins, continues, and ends with attitude—the attitude of Christ (Philippians 2:5–8). That is why we have spent so much time in this study looking at essentials that relate to, and stem from attitude.

Do you have a "good Samaritan" attitude?

For Thought and Discussion

1. How do positive models of God's servants help a deacon understand his ministry better?

   _____

2. Why do we call the Samaritan "Good"?

   _____

3. What was wrong with the attitude and actions of the priest and Levite?

   _____

   _____

4. What do you suppose the lawyer thought as he listened to Jesus tell this parable?

   _____

5. What makes the parable of the good Samaritan unique?

   _____

6. How does the parable relate to helping people stranded on the side of the road in our day?

   _____

7. What motivated the Samaritan to help the robbery victim?

   _____

8. What additional observations do you have about the parable?

   _____

9. How does the parable relate to every Christian?

   _____

10. How do you plan to use this lesson in your ministry?

   _____

→ **CASE STUDY** ←

The Tenth Avenue congregation was planning a series of lessons on the work and qualifications of a deacon. They wanted the series to be different from simply going over the basic texts on the work of deacons, but at the same time they wanted to stay within biblical boundaries. It was suggested that various biblical models of serving, such as the good Samaritan, be used to stress the servant's attitude and heart. Several in the planning meeting were for the proposal and several were against it. Had you been in the meeting, how would you have tried to sell the idea of using Bible models to teach the lesson? Be specific and biblical with your response.

CHAPTER

9

Wanted: Table Servers

NEGLECTED WIDOWS

The church began on the day of Pentecost (Acts 2) and spread like wildfire from the initial conversion of about three thousand souls. The gospel was preached with power, zeal, and simplicity. Luke uses the word *multiply* to describe the rapid growth of the church in the first century. With growth, as we all know, unique issues and challenges arise, such as the one described in Acts 6:1–7. After the church had been in existence for four or five years, the apostles were faced with an issue that related to what we would call the benevolence ministry.

Here is Luke's account of this historical event:

Now in those days, when the number of the disciples was multiplying, there arose a complaint against the Hebrews by the Hellenists, because their widows were neglected in the daily distribution. Then the twelve summoned the multitude of the disciples and said, "It is not desirable that we should leave the word of God and serve tables. Therefore, brethren, seek out from among you seven men of good reputation, full of the Holy Spirit and wisdom, whom we may appoint over this business; but we will give ourselves continually to prayer and to the ministry of the word." And the saying pleased the whole multitude. And they chose Stephen, a man full of faith and the Holy Spirit, and Philip, Prochorus, Nicanor, Timon, Parmenas, and Nicolas, a proselyte from Antioch, whom they set before the apostles; and when they had prayed, they laid hands on them. Then the word of God spread, and the number of the disciples multiplied greatly in Jerusalem, and a great many of the priests were obedient to the faith (Acts 6:1–7).

Fresh from the lying conspiracy of Ananias and Sapphira, which resulted in the first "church funeral" (Acts 5), we come to this problem of discrimination. The Hellenistic Jewish members of the church were murmuring because their widows were neglected or being overlooked.

Prejudice and Discrimination

The Jews had a reputation for their welfare work with the poor and the widows. They maintained a temple fund to help widows, but now that these ladies were members of the Christian community, they could not, or would not, receive these funds. The church evidently had taken up the daily practice of helping the needy. Note that the text does not say the widows were murmuring, but that others were murmuring about their neglect. The complaint seems to have been against the apostles, since they were in charge of the funds that had been contributed (Acts 4:35, 37; 5:2). The disciples had created a disturbance in the church over women and money. Those were very sensitive and possibly explosive issues that needed wisdom.

Those very sensitive and possibly explosive issues needed wisdom.

Just why the Hellenistic widows were being discriminated against, the text does not say. The Jewish people who lived in Palestine proper spoke Aramaic, but many of the Jews who lived outside Palestine spoke Greek—a few spoke Hebrew. Since the Jews who lived outside Palestine freely associated with Greeks, they were resented and thought of as Hellenistic compromisers of their religious principles for financial gain.

When these two diverse groups of Jews were added to the church, it seems that the long-standing negative attitudes between them did not cease. Perhaps the Palestinian Jews had not been liberated from their prejudices, so the problem with the Hellenistic widows arose because the Palestinians resorted to discrimination. We cannot know the reason with certainty, but we do know the problem caused a great stir.

When such delicate problems arise, who are you going to call to help solve it? Where will you find the wisdom, love, and skills to step into such a heated conflict and solve it in the spirit of Christ? The problem would be solved by those apostles who had been personally taught many great lessons about servanthood by Jesus.

It isn't clear how the apostles came to know about the neglected widows. Some writers speculate that they had been waiting on tables, and the job had gotten so involved that they were neglecting their primary mission of praying and ministering in the word. I rather doubt this explanation because the text seems to indicate just the opposite: "It is not desirable that we should leave the word of God and serve tables." That statement seems to prove that they were not serving tables, or if they were, at the most it was probably part time. Whichever case is true, it was time to select some special servants (deacons) to take care of this need. There are kingdom priorities.

THE SELECTION PROCESS

It should be noted that the apostles, in their selection and appointment of special servants, did not do some of the traditional things we do when we select and appoint special servants:

- They didn't ask for volunteers.

- They didn't twist anyone's arm.

- They didn't bribe anyone to serve.

- They didn't give anyone the "we need you" argument or deliver a pressure "pep talk."

- They didn't create "guilt trips."

- They didn't post a "sign up" sheet.

- They didn't use their authority or position to influence.

- They didn't put names before the church and ask for the democratic process of voting to select the deacons.

Although some qualifications are given, the apostles left the method of seeking these men to the discretion of the multitude. The apostles did not reveal a process for us.

The apostles called the congregation together and asked them to choose a "few good men" to serve as deacons over the distribution to widows. *Distribution* is from the Greek *diakonia* and means the same as *serve*. The Greek word *diakonia* or *diakonos* as used here has the same meaning as used in Philippians 1:1 and 1 Timothy 3:8–13; it is usually translated "deacon."

Seek out means that they were to "look at" in order to select men for this work. The entire church was instructed to do this; it was not assigned to a committee. They were to select "from among" themselves "seven men." The number seven sometimes implies completeness, but in this text it doesn't seem to have that significance. Seven men were a sufficient number for handling the work.

THE QUALIFICATIONS

Some have asked why they didn't use the qualifications for deacons as set forth in 1 Timothy 3:8–13. Those qualifications had not been given. The apostle Paul had not written them for Timothy to follow—Paul had not even been converted! The church was still in her early days—probably the first five years—and the number was probably increasing daily. The qualifications the apostles gave were sufficient at that time for those caring for widows. It seems that a permanent set of qualifications was established by Paul for churches to follow.

The basic qualifications were as follows:

1. They were to be males ("seven men").

2. Their character was to be known by the members.

3. They were to have "a good reputation." When investigated, or when their names were brought up, people would speak well of them (Acts 10:22; 16:2; 1 Timothy 5:10).

4. They were to be "full of the Holy Spirit." This phrase no doubt referred to their spirituality, as well as having the "fruit of the Spirit" in their lives (Galatians 5:16–26; Romans 8:1–11). The phrase was also used relative to spiritual gifts (Acts 2:4; 4:8). Men of the flesh couldn't handle the sensitive job of ministering to widows.

5. They were to be men "full . . . of wisdom." They needed to have sound judgment, common sense, and skills in handling touchy situations. Hot-headed or argumentative men couldn't qualify. These needed to be wise men who knew that true wisdom came from God through prayer and experience (James 1:5; 3:13–18). That disqualified novices.

6. They had to be available to serve: "Whom we may appoint over this business." There was a job to be done, not an office to fill. There is no indication that these men were given jurisdiction over any other work or responsibility in the church. They were to wait on tables. Their position was tied to the distribution to widows and would last as long as that need existed.

All the seven men chosen had Greek names. It is assumed that they represented the Hellenistic Jewish Christians in the church. That would insure that the widows would receive proper treatment. No further information is given about these men except for Stephen and Philip.

THE APPOINTMENT

The congregation presented the chosen men to the apostles. This assumes several things:

♦ The apostles considered the church mature enough to select these men.

♦ The apostles didn't want the sole responsibility for selecting these men. Perhaps they didn't know the church well enough. The congregation knew each other in an intimate way (cf. 1 Corinthians 12:13–27). They were together in daily fellowship (Acts 2:44–47). There was no stranger among them.

♦ The apostles accepted the choices of the church.

Once the seven men were set before the apostles, prayers were offered and the apostles laid hands on them. The text is not clear whether the whole congregation prayed or only the twelve. The laying on of hands was of the apostles' hands. That act was symbolic. It had no mystical power, but was the gesture of setting these men apart for the specific work of waiting on tables. It wasn't to receive the Holy Spirit; they already had the Spirit. This ritual was not the same as the rabbinic ordination where some special "charisma" was transmitted by the act of laying on of hands.

Hotheaded or argumentative men couldn't qualify.

There is no indication in Scripture that this historical narrative of how the Jerusalem church met a specific need is bound on all congregations. It may, however, be used as a model for meeting needs. When Paul later gave Timothy instructions for deacons, he didn't mention or incorporate these requirements. Some say we should combine them. Then we would have the complete picture of the work of deacons, their qualifications, and how to select them.

When needs are met in a scriptural way, the gospel advances.

THE RESULTS

After the apostles had properly handled the problem of discrimination, the strife in the church ended: "Then the word of God continued to spread, and the number of the disciples multiplied greatly in Jerusalem, and a great many of the priests were obedient to the faith" (Acts 6:7). When needs are met in a scriptural way, as they were in the Jerusalem church, the gospel advances. When a congregation is bogged down in issues and persons are neglecting their ministries, the cause of Christ suffers.

It is still true that people outside the church are impressed when they see a spirit of love and harmony, rather than a spirit of division and fussing. In a spirit of harmony our Christian lights shine brighter, making us more attractive to friends who need the Savior.

FOR THOUGHT AND DISCUSSION

1. When the problem arose with the Grecian widows, how long had the church been established?

2. Why do problems usually accompany rapid growth?

3. The King James Version uses the word *murmuring* in Acts 6:1. What does *murmur* mean?

4. Who was murmuring?

_____

5. How do you suppose the widows were being neglected?

_____

6. Why didn't the apostles choose the deacons?

_____

7. How do you suppose the church was able to select these seven men?

_____

8. Discuss their qualifications. How, if at all, are those qualification bound today?

_____

_____

9. What additional observations do you have?

_____

10. How do you plan to use this lesson?

_____

→ CASE STUDY ←

The Valley congregation was trying to decide how to use the historical narrative in Acts 6 in the ordination of deacons. Some suggested that they should pray and fast; others suggested that they should shake hands instead of placing hands on the shoulders of the chosen men; a few suggested that they should avoid the word *ordain*. If you were asked your opinion in this matter, what advice would you give to help them make proper decisions in appointing their new deacons? Be specific and biblical in your answers.

CHAPTER

10

God's Expectations of Deacons

What Not to Be

After nine lessons, it should be clear that God's idea of what is involved in being a deacon may be different from what some brethren or congregations believe. By way of reminder, God does not want deacons in local churches so they can:

1. be "office holders."

2. "run the affairs of the church."

3. serve as "junior elders" (equal to vice presidents).

4. sit in judgment on all programs of the church.

5. conduct their "own little business."

6. be involved in every ministry.

7. have something to do that will keep them busy.

8. be elevated above the rest of the congregation.

9. politick for a pet issue or program.

10. create unrest and uneasiness because of their attitudes and remarks toward their ministry.

> *Deacons were chosen because there was a specific need.*

From the brief model presented in Acts 6, we see that deacons were chosen because there was a specific need: the widows were being neglected. There were not to be any deacons sitting in an office somewhere waiting for a job or a need to arise so they could go to work. The need is first, and then servants are selected to do it. The Bible doesn't exemplify a deacon's being appointed without a work to do, as so frequently happens today. The Bible is silent about what happens to a selected deacon once his work assignment is completed. I recognize that we must be careful about making arguments on the silence of Scriptures, but it seems to me that if his work has ceased, according to biblical examples, there would be no need for him to serve as a deacon.

BIBLICAL QUALIFICATIONS

While the Bible clearly teaches that all Christians are to be servants, it also clearly teaches that there are some ministries that require special kind of servants, persons called deacons (Acts 6:1–7), who must meet the qualifications given by God in the Bible.

The qualifications for deacons follow the qualifications given by Paul for elders in 1 Timothy, where Paul wrote, "Likewise deacons must . . . ," thus showing there is a distinction between the two works. Here is the whole text:

> Likewise deacons must be reverent, not double-tongued, not given to much wine, not greedy for money, holding the mystery of the faith with a pure conscience. But let these also first be tested; then let them serve as deacons, being found blameless. Likewise their wives be reverent, not slanderers, temperate, faithful in all things. Let deacons be the husbands of one wife, ruling their children and their own houses well. For those who have served well as deacons obtain for themselves a good standing and great boldness in the faith which is in Christ Jesus (1 Timothy 3:8–13).

Some scholars believe Paul wrote these remarks some twenty-five years after the establishment of the church—twenty years after the Jerusalem problem over widows. By then there must have been a need for uniformity in the selection and appointment of deacons. Paul was selected by the Holy Spirit to give these to Timothy, the young evangelist, who in turn would share them with churches. They have come down to us today in the Bible.

A CLOSER LOOK AT THE QUALIFICATIONS
Let's take a more in-depth look at the qualifications given by Paul.

❖ QUALIFICATIONS OF 1 TIMOTHY 3:8–13 ❖

◆ *A deacon must be "reverent."* This is an emphasis on his dignity as a Christian who has a respectable reputation in spiritual matters. He is not a clown or wise-cracker at the expense of others. This doesn't mean that he is a stoic, but rather he has a mature quality that produces a balanced life. He is a serious thinker who takes his ministry in the church seriously (Proverbs 23:7). A deacon is worthy of respect because he is a man of high principles (Philippians 4:8; Titus 2:2).

◆ *A deacon must not be "double-tongued."* This means that he is not two-faced; he does not speak out of both sides of his mouth, saying one thing in one place and another in a different context. He must not be a gossip who spreads tales among those to whom he ministers. As he goes from house to house, he must be "speaking the truth in love" (Ephesians 4:15). He is not a liar, but an honest, straight-forward servant of God. His yes is yes and his no is no. You can trust what he says. He follows the proverb to "buy the truth, and do not sell it" (Proverbs 23:23). A deacon must be sincere and free from hypocrisy.

◆ *A deacon must not be "given to much wine."* He must not be addicted to alcoholic beverages or enslaved by their power. Such usage is out of harmony with the conduct of a mature servant striving to imitate Christ. He must be "pure in heart" (Matthew 5:8), which means his mind is not polluted by intoxicating drink. I think we are safe in extending this prohibition to the usage of illegal drugs or anything that demonstrates an inappropriate dependence on any substance. A deacon must strive to be "an example to the believers in word, in conduct, in love, in spirit, in faith, in purity" (1 Timothy 4:12).

◆ *A deacon must not be "greedy for money."* The deacon is in a position, if he so chooses, to make money from his services. As he circulates among the brethren, he is privileged to know many things that could be turned into his financial advantage. He is not serving in order to line his pockets or gain in financial favors (Titus 1:7). Deacons are to be honest in all things. They have learned the lesson that "it is more blessed to give than to receive" (Acts 20:35). A deacon in charge of church finances is potentially faced with special temptation. He must give considerable thought as to how he handles God's money. Likewise, a deacon may have to give up his desire to make money in order to serve tables. That quality relates to a personal value system, which is very important to serving as a deacon. A deacon is a good steward (1 Corinthians 4:1–2).

◆ *A deacon must be a man who is "holding the mystery of the faith with a pure conscience."* He must know the truth and have no doubts about what he believes. Paul uses the "mystery of the faith" to refer to the eternal scheme of redemption that has been revealed through the gospel (Ephesians 1:3–12; 1 Timothy 3:9; Romans 16:25). Paul identifies what this mystery is in 1 Timothy 3:16. Jude reminds us that "the faith" must be contended for by making a defense (Jude 3). "Holding the mystery" means he will not compromise the truth (John 8:32), and "pure conscience" means he believes what he knows and is a doer of the word (James 1:22). He is a consistent servant who safeguards the truth. This also seems to imply that he is not a novice (Hebrews 5:12–6:2).

◆ *A deacon must "first be tested."* The word *tested* means to be proved. It was used to describe the testing of metal to prove its strength and reliability. (Note Paul's usage in other places: 1 Thessalonians 2:4; Philippians 1:10.) There are no details given as to how this testing or proving is to be carried out. I believe it refers to determining whether or not a man is qualified to serve in the particular ministry for which he has been recommended. Just as a man must prove he can fly an airplane before he is hired as a pilot, a deacon must demonstrate that he can serve in a certain position before he is officially assigned to that job. This means that we don't just suspect that the person being appointed has the ability to be a deacon; his ability has already been proved. Before being appointed to serve as a deacon, a man must undergo careful scrutiny.

◆ *Once a deacon has been proved, he is then "appointed to the work."* He is not first appointed to serve and then trained. He has already qualified when he is appointed. That method eliminates the "generic pool" consisting of men who are ready to be appointed as deacons and then be trained for any work that may come up.

◆ *Another attribute of a deacon is "blameless."* He has a good reputation in character, skills, and spirituality. He does not lack the qualities needed to carry out his ministry assignment. There is a different Greek word used of elders in 1 Timothy 3:2, but the same word is used in Titus 1:6.

◆ *A deacon must be "the husband of one wife."* This means that the deacon must be married. He is to have only one wife; he must not be a polygamist or living in an adulterous, unscriptural marriage. The same qualification is required of an elder (1 Timothy 3:2). The deacon must honor his wife as Christ loves and honors the church (Ephesians 5:25–33). Servanthood begins at home with the family.

◆ *A deacon must be "able to rule his children."* This means that he must have children, but it seems "believing children" are not required of him as they are required of an elder. But since fathers are to take the lead in educating and training their children, the deacon's children must be obedient to him (Ephesians 6:1–4). If a deacon cannot control his children, how can he successfully minister in the work of the Lord? Managing his children well demonstrates his ability to get along with people.

◆ *The deacon must "rule his house well."* His domestic abilities extend to all areas of managing household affairs. By showing his ability to manage the household, he is demonstrating the ability to manage his ministry assignment. This means that a deacon is organized, self-disciplined, and knowledgeable about what needs to be done. He does things decently and in order. His management proving ground is his own home. An investigation—he must first be tested—will reveal his proficiency in this qualification.

◆ *A deacon must "have served well."* That is an added emphasis on his desire, abilities, and the carrying out of his assignment. He is not sidetracked;

neither does he use his status as a deacon for reasons other than what he was appointed to do. He is not a servant who is merely trying to get by with doing the minimum. Whatever his hands find to do, he does it with all his might.

◆ *A deacon who serves well "obtains for himself a good standing."* This relates to the blessing of being approved, appointed, and empowered to do the work of ministry. The Greek text places an emphasis on "being in good standing," and the phrase was used to describe a person who has climbed the stairs and has reached the place of sure footedness, not in authority, but in being recognized as having done his work acceptably. This speaks of the personal reward or satisfaction of doing his ministry properly. He feels good about what he has done.

◆ *A deacon will also be blessed with "great boldness in the faith."* One cannot be bashful or shy in his work as a deacon; neither must he be harsh or unkind in his ministry. God does not approve of cowards in His service (2 Timothy 1:7; Revelation 21:8). Their boldness relates to the faith—the gospel—the ministry of the Lord. Boldness was one of the characteristics of the disciples in the first century (Acts 4:13, 19–20, 29, 31; 9:29; 13:46). As a deacon goes about his ministry, he is involved in sharing the faith with those to whom he ministers. He knows that everyone needs to hear the gospel (Mark 16:15–16). He does not limit himself to waiting on tables. As a Christian he also has a responsibility to the *Great Commission.* Stephen and Philip once served tables (Acts 6:1–7). They later became bold and powerful defenders and sharers of the faith (Acts 7–8). A deacon's boldness stems from his relationship with Jesus Christ. That is his only motivation (Philippians 2:5–8).

A GOOD STANDING

The Scripture reveals that the work of a deacon is very important. While all Christians are servants, a deacon is qualified to serve in special ministries, and must, therefore, meet specific qualifications as outlined in the Bible.

Contrary to the thinking of some, the deacon doesn't use his position as a steppingstone to be an elder. The two works are very different and a particular deacon may never qualify to be an elder.

Deacons have assignments that they must perform efficiently and effectively. They are able to do so because they were proved to have the ability before they were assigned to the ministry task.

When a deacon has done his work well, he has obtained for himself "a good standing and great boldness in the faith which is in Christ Jesus" (1 Timothy 3:13). Thank God for these great servants who serve the Lord and His church.

FOR THOUGHT AND DISCUSSION

1. Why weren't the qualifications given in 1 Timothy used in the appointment of deacons in Acts 6?

2. Why do we need biblical authority for deacons?

3. Why is there sometimes confusion about the work and authority of deacons?

4. Does the meaning of the word *deacon* suggest the kind of work he does?

5. What is the relationship, biblically speaking, between elders and deacons?

6. In what sense is the deacon not an "office holder"?

7. What are the limitations on the kinds of ministries in which a deacon may serve? Why?

8. How does a congregation go about proving whether or not a prospective deacon can do a certain work?

_____

9. What are some of the ministry assignments a deacon may perform?

_____

_____

_____

10. What additional observations do you have?

_____

_____

→ **CASE STUDY** ←

Fred had been a member of the Broad Street church for several years. It was rumored that he was thinking about moving his membership to a congregation across town where he could serve as a deacon. When the elders got wind of this, they called Fred into a meeting and offered to make him a deacon. You have been asked to give advice in this matter. How would you approach it biblically? Be specific in your answers, as well as biblical.

CHAPTER

11

Welcome to the Team

GOD'S "CHAIN GANG"

When a man is appointed to serve as a deacon, he usually becomes part of an existing group of deacons, elders, teachers, and preachers. This is God's "chain gang"—His cadre of slaves. Each, as a member of the body of Christ, has a function to perform (Ephesians 4:11–16; 1 Corinthians 12:12–31). In twenty-first-century language we call this group a team.

With the team concept we shift our emphasis to doing the work of a deacon in an orderly and expedient manner. This concept is vital in a society that promotes individualism or "doing your own thing." Only at Burger King may a deacon have it his way. In the church it must be God's way, and God's way is unity and cooperation (Ephesians 4:1–7).

During an interview about his great performance with a championship football team, the quarterback said, "It was a total team effort. Every man played his spot absolutely perfectly . . . It was a team effort, from the coaches, front office, water boys . . . everybody had a part in the win." What a team player! What a great attitude. What a great lesson for Christians!

> *Only at Burger King may a deacon have it his way.*

We spend our lives in groups and teams. Some of these have been highly organized and productive; others have been loosely organized, with few objectives. When we were kids we had "our gang." In a more visible sense, our awareness of teams stem from their coverage in the news media, where their results (productions) are presented. When a man is appointed to serve as a deacon, he usually becomes part of a team in the local church. He becomes a team player.

BIBLICAL EMPHASIS ON TEAMS

Since teams are vital to the growth of the church, we are not surprised to see numerous examples of teams in the Bible. Remember, a team is a number of people, two or more, who are organized to function cooperatively as a group toward a common objective. The objectives of the team will determine how it functions. Here are some Bible examples of teams:

1. The Godhead—Father, Son, and Holy Spirit—is a perfect team (Matthew 28:18–20).

2. Jethro and Moses. (Exodus 18:13–24 gives advice for team-building.)

3. Ten of the twelve spies (Numbers 13–14). (Note: Joshua and Caleb were a different team.)

4. David's mighty men (1 Chronicles 12:32; men of Issachar, cf. 7:5).

5. Jesus and His disciples (Mark 1:14–20).

6. Paul and his followers (Acts 15:32–39, team problems).

7. Aquila and Priscilla, a husband and wife team (Acts 18:24–28).

8. Teams we should build:
   ◆ Elders (Titus 1:5; 1 Timothy 3:1–7).
   ◆ Deacons (Acts 6:1–7; 1 Timothy 3:8–13).
   ◆ Teachers (Hebrews 5:12; Ephesians 4:11–16).
   ◆ Partners with God (1 Corinthians 3:4–9).

9. Examples of a team functioning (Acts 15:5–12).

10. Example of elders functioning as a team (James 5:14–16; Acts 20:17–38).

Today when a church forms teams, it is well within Bible principles and examples in doing so. The challenge is to form them properly for the carrying out of the church's mission. Deacons play a vital role in the organization and function of ministry teams.

Local Church Teams

Most congregations, depending on the size of the membership, have some of these teams (groups) functioning in them:

- Elders
- Deacons
- Teachers
- Ministry leaders
- Church staffs
- Visitation teams

- Ladies groups
- Teen groups
- Singles groups
- Young marrieds
- Middle-adults
- Senior-adults

Deacons may be involved in most of these teams, either from a leadership position or in a participation role. The challenge is to develop all these small groups into productive elements in the larger team. God uses the analogy of the human body to teach us just how we should function as a team—"many members, yet one body." (See 1 Corinthians 12:12–31.)

How to Build a Team

As team leaders, deacons need to know some of the major things that need to be acted upon in order to have an effective team. This knowledge will help them delegate to team members. Here is a brief listing of some priority things deacons need to know regarding the building of their ministry team:

1. The team must know the priority given by God. (The kingdom is the priority.) (Matthew 6:33).

2. The team must know what the "Father's business" is (Luke 2:49).

3. The team must know what God's vision is for the church (Isaiah 2:2–4; Mark 16:15–16):
   - Evangelism (Mark 16:15–16; Matthew 28:18–20).
   - Edification of the church (Ephesians 4:11–16).
   - Benevolence: helping those who are in need (Galatians 6:10; James 1:27).
   - Developing leadership (Titus 1:5–9; 1 Timothy 3:1–13; Acts 6:1–7).
   - Worshiping God "in spirit and truth" (John 4:24).
   - Stewardship: proper use of money, life, abilities (1 Corinthians 4:1–2).
   - Preparing members to be teachers (Hebrews 5:12–14).
   - Training and skills development for servants in the church.

4. The team must know the importance of each member of the body:
   - 1 Corinthians 12:12–31.
   - Ephesians 4:11–16.
   - Romans 12:3–8.

5. The team must know the biblical nature of the church:
   - The builder is Christ (Matthew 16:14–19).
   - The head is Christ (Colossians 1:18).
   - The saved are in the church (1 Corinthians 12:18; Acts 2:47).
   - The church is the bride of Christ (Ephesians 5; Revelation 19).
   - The church is the pillar and ground of the truth (1 Timothy 3:15).
   - God is glorified through the church (Ephesians 3:21).

6. The team must be aware of its responsibility to followers:
   - 1 Timothy 4:12.
   - Matthew 5:13–16.
   - Matthew 23:3–5.

7. The team must be committed to faithfulness (Revelation 2:10; Hebrews 11:1–6).

In this lesson we have sought to focus on the participation of a deacon in a team effort in the local church. Ministry doesn't take place in isolation. It is a cooperative effort requiring each servant to do his part. Somebody has to pitch, play first base, play in the outfield—somebody has to play every other position, if the team hopes to win. Somebody has to do every work in the kingdom in order for us to be successful in the mission God has given to the church.

I know of some congregations where the right hand doesn't know what the left hand is doing. Such disorganization produces conflict, unrest, and neglect between deacons and other team members—elders, teachers, and preachers.

For Thought and Discussion

1. How does the work of a deacon relate to the team concept of leadership?

   _____

2. How does communication relate to team participation?

   _____

3. How effective will a "Lone Ranger" deacon be?

   _____

4. How is the best way to organize a team?

   _____

5. What are some of the teams that function in your congregation?

   _____

   _____

6. How may a team work more efficiently?

   _____

   _____

7. What additional teams does your congregation need?

   _____

8. List some things that weaken a team?

   _____

   _____

9. How do you feel about your position on the team?

   _____

10. What additional observations do you have?

    _____

    _____

Bill was appointed an elder of the Newport congregation. One of the first things he tried to do was to organize the various ministries into teams, with a deacon in charge of each. Several of the deacons resisted, expressing that they thought things were all right the way they were. How would you have tried to sell the opposing deacons on the need for developing teams? Be biblical and specific in your answers.

Your Attitude Is Showing

THE FRUIT OF THOUGHTS

The wise man said, "For as he thinks in his heart, so is he" (Proverbs 23:7). God promised to give His people the "fruit of their thoughts" (Jeremiah 6:19). A deacon's attitude will determine the nature of his service to God and the local church.

Henry: "What's your attitude toward work?"
Chester: Oh, it doesn't bother me. I can sit and watch."

Henry: "What's your attitude toward work?"
Burt: "I do just enough to get by."

Henry: "What's your attitude toward work?"
Phil: "I never have enough time to finish."

Henry: "What's your attitude toward work?"
Will: "I believe in a full-day's work for a full-day's pay."

Henry: "What's your attitude toward work?
You: _____

Ministry—the work of a deacon—means serving God, and serving God means doing the work you have been assigned. Sadly, in the church there seems to be two extremes: idler—workaholic.

God has not called us to either of these extremes. He wants us to give our best, while at the same time maintaining a balanced lifestyle. This is why attitude plays a major role in the work of a deacon. A deacon's attitude at the beginning of a project, as a rule, will determine the outcome of the effort.

WORK ETHICS

Regardless of the job, business, or vocation, most works have ethics tied to them. These are norms that set forth standards of accountability, responsibilities, and production quotas. *Work ethic* is also a term that is applied to characteristics of people, both at work and play. In sports, for example, work ethic is frequently mentioned as an outstanding quality in a successful player. Regardless of the context, work ethic is usually associated with people who work hard and do a good job.

As a general rule the characteristics of an approved work ethic involves:

◆ the worker's attitude.

◆ the worker's interpersonal skills.

◆ initiative on the job.

◆ being dependable.

◆ accomplishing the task according to directions.

◆ making a positive contribution to the objectives of the company.

◆ how well one works without the need for immediate supervision.

◆ how resources are handled.

◆ commitment to employment agreement.

◆ job satisfaction.

Here are some major categories that represent vocations for research purposes. Take a minute and think about what the work ethics and initiatives are in each of these categories:

◆ Medical professionals (doctor, dentist, psychiatrist).

◆ Other professionals (teacher, lawyer, accountant, social worker, minister).

- ◆ Services (waitress, construction worker, cashier, plumber).

- ◆ Sales (insurance, auto, real estate, department store).

- ◆ Full-time homemakers (cook, cleaner, hostess).

- ◆ Unemployed (looking for work, welfare).

Thinking in these categories automatically opens the door to the ministry and work of a deacon. The church is composed of servants (workers) who have the world's greatest ethics to follow—the Word of God. A deacon's attitude toward these standards will determine how he works in the Lord's vineyard.

THE BIBLE AND WORK ETHICS

There are numerous passages in the Bible that set forth God's requirements for work and ministry. Knowledge and application of these will create an attitude adjustment, if needed, in deacons toward their ministry in the church.

→ GOD'S WORK REQUIREMENTS ←

- ◆ God has required man to work from the beginning of creation (Genesis 2:15).

- ◆ God requires that we work fervently at any task we undertake (Ecclesiastes 9:10).

- ◆ God demands that we be diligent to receive His approval (2 Timothy 2:15).

- ◆ God doesn't want us to work only when being watched (Ephesians 6:5–8).

- ◆ God does not approve of laziness (Proverbs 19:15; Ecclesiastes 10:18).

- ◆ God will reward us according to our work (Matthew 16:27).

- ◆ God wants us to be fruitful in every good work (Colossians 1:10).

- ◆ God knows our works (Revelation 2:2).

- ◆ God wants us to finish what we start (Revelation 2:10; Ecclesiastes 7:8).

◆ God has chosen us to be working partners with Him (1 Corinthians 3:9; 2 Corinthians 6:1–2).

◆ God will test our works (1 Corinthians 3:12–15).

◆ God doesn't want deceitful workers (2 Corinthians 11:13).

A man had a dream in which he imagined his own death and being taken by the angels to a beautiful temple. After admiring it for a time he discovered that one little stone was left out. "Why was this stone left out?" he asked the angel. "That was left out for you," replied the angel, "but you wanted to do great things, so there was no room left for you." The man awoke startled, and resolved that he would become a worker for God. After that, he always worked faithfully, even in small things.

> Work as if you will live a hundred years.
> Pray as if you will die tomorrow.
> —Ben Franklin

> The smallest deed is better
> Than the greatest intention!
> —Unknown

What is Your Level of Involvement in Ministry?
(Indicate on scale below)
Not involved 1 2 3 4 5 6 7 8 9 10 Totally involved

What do you plan to do as a deacon to become more involved in the Lord's work?

SELF-EXAMINATION

Deacons are not exempt from what God has told us to *be* and what He has told us to *do*. On the following scale, indicate where you believe you are in *doing* the good works God wants you to do as a deacon:

1. My level of maturity as a Christian is:
   Poor 1 2 3 4 5 6 7 8 9 10 Excellent

2. My level of involvement in teaching the lost is:
   Poor 1 2 3 4 5 6 7 8 9 10 Excellent

3. My level of involvement as a deacon or a servant is:
   Poor 1 2 3 4 5 6 7 8 9 10 Excellent

4. My fruit bearing is:
   Poor 1 2 3 4 5 6 7 8 9 10 Excellent

5. My attitude as a team player is:
   Poor 1 2 3 4 5 6 7 8 9 10 Excellent

6. My level of glorifying God in my work is:
   Poor 1 2 3 4 5 6 7 8 9 10 Excellent

7. My level of being a doer of the word is:
   Poor 1 2 3 4 5 6 7 8 9 10 Excellent

In the spirit of Paul, may we all say after this self-examination:

"Brethren, I do not regard myself as having laid hold of it yet; but one thing I do: forgetting what lies behind and reaching forward to what lies ahead, I press on toward the goal for the prize of the upward call of God in Christ Jesus" (Philippians 3:13–14 NASB).

It's all about attitude—the attitude of Christ!

STIMULATING QUESTIONS FOR DEACON TEAM MEMBERS

Take a few minutes and answer yes or no to the following remarks, remembering *effectiveness* is getting the results God wants:

Biblically, can I be an effective team member and . . .

_____ not glorify God?

_____ not support the team?

_____ not do my job?

_____ complain all the time?

_____ not follow the rules?

_____ refuse to help?

_____ not be a team player?

_____ not be accountable?
_____ harm the team by constant criticism?
_____ not cooperate?
_____ not attend team meetings?
_____ do my own thing?
_____ undermine the work?
_____ not be qualified?
_____ drag my feet?
_____ be negative continually?
_____ sabotage a competing work or team?
_____ not pray?
_____ not follow the Scripture?
_____ not walk by faith?
_____ not sacrifice?
_____ not have a Christ-like attitude?
_____ not be a good example to others?
_____ be afraid or live in fear of failure?
_____ never improve my skills?
_____ not be well organized?
_____ not study my Bible?
_____ worry too much about what people think?
_____ be afraid to make decisions?
_____ be content to remain status quo?
_____ never evaluate my progress?
_____ never take positive action toward my goals?
_____ have a closed mind to new ideas?
_____ never delegate?
_____ never admit my own weaknesses or faults?
_____ be stubborn and self-willed?
_____ have a hidden agenda?

All of these questions and how you answer them reflect an attitude and a need. What has it revealed about your needs and attitudes as a deacon?

FOR THOUGHT AND DISCUSSION

1. Define *attitude.*

   _____

2. Why is a deacon's attitude important?

   _____

3. Define *ethic.* How does it relate to the work of a deacon?

   _____

   _____

4. How is a deacon a team member?

   _____

5. How does attitude relate to team participation?

   _____

6. How do the Bible examples of work ethics relate to the work of a deacon?

   _____

7. What is your present level of involvement in ministry?

   _____

8. Review the self-examination exercise. Discuss.

   _____

   _____

9. What additional observations do you have?

   _____

   _____

10. How may a deacon improve his attitude?

    _____

    _____

→ **CASE STUDY** ←

The morale of the deacons at the Fifth Street congregation was very low. Some had slacked off on their assignments, a few were pointing fingers, and general unrest was obvious. Two deacons had resigned and others were threatening to follow suit. You have been asked to address the problem. How would you use the biblical teaching on attitudes and thinking to develop a possible solution to the problem? Be biblical and specific in your solutions.

Deacons and Delegation

FRUSTRATIONS OF DELEGATION

Some frequently heard complaints of deacons:

1. "The elders don't trust me."

2. "The elders are always looking over my shoulder."

3. "I don't have authority to spend any money."

4. "I don't have a job description."

5. "I am treated like a novice . . . no respect."

6. "The elders are doing my work."

7. "The elders never communicate with me."

8. "All the elders do is get in my way as I try to do my job."

9. "I don't know how I am doing; the elders never discuss or evaluate my work with me."

10. "The elders give me the ball, but then when I run too fast they tackle me."

As a whole, these remarks relate to the frustrations deacons feel regarding delegation. Complaints about delegation—usually the lack of it—are what I have heard most frequently from deacons across the brotherhood.

In order for a deacon to do his work effectively, he must be empowered to do so. That empowerment comes from (1) his desire to do the work, (2) his qualifications to do the work, (3) his abilities to do the work, and (4) delegation to do the work.

> *No leader can be a one-man show! Not even Moses.*

What is delegation? Webster defines *delegate* as: "to entrust (authority, power, etc.) to a person acting as one's agent or representative." Good delegation doesn't happen by chance or accident. It takes awareness of what needs to be done, the selection of the right person to do the job, and delegating to the person authority to do whatever it takes to accomplish the task.

There are numerous implications involved in delegation. Delegation implies respect for someone else's abilities to accomplish a task. Delegation involves taking a risk. You are trusting another to do something important. When you delegate, you are sharing a workload and responsibility. Likewise, delegation involves responsibility and accountability.

BIBLE EXAMPLES OF DELEGATION

There are numerous outstanding examples of delegation in God's Word. A study of them will give us deeper insight into this great need in the church, especially with regards to the ministry of deacons.

MOSES

One of the clearest accounts of the need for delegation and the actual delegation process is recorded in Exodus 18. In this context Moses has been trying to do all the work himself; he is not only wearing himself out but the people as well. His work is from morning until the evening.

In the midst of the workday, Moses' father-in-law shows up and observes what Moses is doing with the people. Jethro asks his son-in-law, "What is this thing that you are doing for the people? Why do you alone sit, and all the people stand before you from morning until evening?" (Exodus 18:14).

After Moses answers Jethro's question, Jethro goes out on a limb with his son-in-law and says, "The thing that you do is not good. Both you and these people who are with you will surely wear yourselves out. For this thing is too much for you; you are not able to perform it by yourself" (Exodus 18:17–18).

No leader can be a one-man show! Not even Moses.

Jethro has not finished giving advice to Moses. He proposes a method of finding men and authorizing them to act as judges. Jethro advises Moses:

> Moreover you shall select from all the people able men, such as fear God, men of truth, hating covetousness; and place such over them to be rulers of thousands, rulers of hundreds, rulers of fifties, and rulers of tens. And let them judge the people at all times. Then it will be that every great matter they shall bring to you, but every small matter they themselves shall judge. So it will be easier for you, for they will bear the burden with you (Exodus 18:21–22).

The rest of Exodus 18 shows how Moses obeys the instructions of Jethro and delegates the work among approved men.

Every great leader needs help, and the best way to get it is to find qualified men and delegate some of the work to them.

JESUS

Jesus left heaven and came to earth to minister (Mark 10:45). One of His core objectives was the selection, training, empowering, and commissioning of His apostles to carry on His work after He went back to heaven.

In Mark's Gospel we have this account: "And as he walked by the Sea of Galilee, He saw Simon and Andrew his brother casting a net into the sea; for they were fishermen. Then Jesus said to them, 'Follow Me, and I will make you become fishers of men.' They immediately left their nets and followed Him" (Mark 1:16–18).

In Jesus' dynamic prayer recorded by John, we have a very detailed description of how Jesus chose, empowered, and delegated to the apostles (John 17:8–26).

Jesus chose, empowered, and delegated to His apostles.

The *Great Commission* is another clear account of Jesus delegating to His apostles. He said,

> All authority has been given to Me in heaven and on earth. Go therefore and make disciples of all the nations, baptizing them in the name of the Father and of the Son and of the Holy Spirit, teaching them to observe all things that I have commanded you; and lo, I am with you always, even to the end of the age (Matthew 28:18–20).

What an awesome delegation! To be Christ's representatives on earth; to carry on His work; and to train (delegate to) others to do likewise. It has come down to us for continuance.

THE APOSTLES

As we have already noticed in our study, the apostles directed the church in Jerusalem to select seven men whom the apostles might appoint as deacons over the distribution of goods to widows (Acts 6:1–7). The apostles' primary work was in the Word and in prayer, so they needed men to serve tables. Nobody can do everything, not even the apostles. Neither can one deacon!

We have another example of delegation, as Paul gave instructions to Timothy for training teachers: "You therefore, my son, be strong in the grace that is in Christ Jesus. And the things that you have heard from me among many witnesses, commit these to faithful men who will be able to teach others also" (2 Timothy 2:1–2).

From the actions of Moses, Jesus, and Paul we have learned that the Bible exemplifies delegations. We must learn to do the same thing. In fact, the selection and appointment of deacons is based upon the principle of delegating work to capable men.

A CLOSER LOOK AT DELEGATION

It is necessary for us to take a closer look at what is involved in delegating.

✧ WHAT DELEGATION IS NOT ✧

1. Getting someone to do the "dirty work."

2. "Passing the buck."

3. "Letting George do it."

4. Making "busy-work" for a deacon.

5. Creating something to keep a deacon "faithful."

6. Establishing a "Sail your own ship" agenda.

7. Exercising power over someone.

8. Making a nebulous assignment.

9. Remaining void of authority and accountability.

10. Giving someone an unimportant responsibility.

⤳ WHAT DELEGATING INVOLVES ⬳

1. Awareness of a need for help.

2. Selection of a qualified person.

3. Commitment to the ministry.

4. Trust—both sides.

5. Stewardship of time, talent, and finances.

6. Team effort.

7. Fulfillment of a responsibility.

8. Specific work.

9. Patience and cooperation.

10. Authority and resources.

⤳ KEYS TO EFFECTIVE DELEGATING ⬳

1. Begin with a clearly defined objective in mind when selecting the person for a job.

2. Have a clearly defined set of skills needed to do the job effectively.

3. Choose the person who has a proven record for doing a good job (1 Timothy 3:10).

4. Communicate standards of performance expected.

5. Make available the necessary resources.

6. Conduct a training program to equip the person, if special training is necessary.

7. Establish a reasonable timeline for completion, if the task is terminal.

8. Put in place a clearly defined reporting-of-progress system—dates, what, how, when, and who.

9. Present a clearly defined monitoring plan.

10. Clearly define a set of guidelines for evaluating job progress and performance.

11. Agree on the procedure for terminating the program or terminating the deacon's involvement in it.

12. Provide opportunities for continuing education to ensure skills and growth.

✦ How to Handle Delegated Assignments ✦

1. Be committed to the task for which you accept responsibility.

2. Finish what you start (Ecclesiastes 7:8).

3. Have the right attitude (Philippians 2:5–8).

4. Do your work with zeal (Colossians 3:23).

5. Don't look back once you start (Luke 9:62).

6. Remember, you are a worker with God (2 Corinthians 6:1–2).

7. Be a faithful steward (1 Corinthians 4:2).

8. Pray continually for wisdom (James 1:1–5).

9. Get organized for efficient work.

10. Seek advice; get help from others; delegate.

11. Be a self-disciplined deacon (2 Peter 1:6).

12. Be an example to others (1 Timothy 4:12).

13. Don't grumble, bad-mouth, or complain.

14. Keep the kingdom first in your life and ministry (Matthew 6:33).

15. Never quit or throw in the towel (Revelation 2:10).

Because of the way the Lord's church is organized, it is imperative that persons, especially deacons, be given clearly defined areas of responsibility. That requires careful and prayerful delegation. In this study we have noted the importance of delegation in the Bible. If Moses, Jesus, the apostles, and Timothy needed to delegate, how can we get by without it? We cannot!

> *It is imperative that deacons be given clearly defined responsibility.*

Not only must deacons be assigned specific ministries, they must also be given the authority to carry out their jobs, and this includes the funds for getting the job done. If the practical suggestions in this chapter are followed, both sides in delegation will function more effectively in the Lord's work. More things will get done and followers will be happier. You cannot not delegate!

FOR THOUGHT AND DISCUSSION

1. What is delegation?

2. Why are some deacons frustrated over delegation issues?

3. Why do some elderships do a poor job of delegating work?

4. How do you feel about the way responsibility has been delegated to you?

5. Discuss Moses and delegation. What are the major lessons from the narrative in Exodus 18?

6. Discuss some additional ways Jesus delegated.

7. Why are some elderships afraid to delegate?

8. What is a good agenda to follow when delegating?

9. What is the biggest problem with delegation in your congregation?

10. What additional observations do you have?

The Westside congregation is having a leadership meeting which involves the elders, deacons, preachers, and ministry leaders. One of the deacons brings up the subject of delegaton. Accusations ring out, tempers begin to heat up, and problems begin to brew in the meeting. You are given the floor to make suggestions as to how to improve the delegation among the deacons and all team members. What will be your approach? Be specific and biblical in your answer.

Wanted: Deacons Who Will Serve Joyfully

WHY WE NEED DEACONS TO SERVE JOYFULLY

There are numerous reasons we need twenty-first-century deacons to serve joyfully. One of these reasons is based on the challenges faced by all leaders in the church, especially elders, deacons, and preachers. Study very carefully and prayerfully the following challenges.

⇾ CHALLENGES OF LEADERSHIP ⇽

- ◆ Unprecedented ignorance of the Scripture (Hosea 4:6–8).

- ◆ Apathy toward the mission of the church (John 4:35–36).

- ◆ An indifferent attitude toward getting involved in church activities (1 Samuel 17:29).

- ◆ A separatist mindset of some members—no concept of church family (1 Corinthians 12:12–31).

- ◆ Poor and inadequate leadership skills.

- ◆ Post-modernism thinking and attitudes, both in and out of the church.

- ◆ Diverse cultural challenges, both in the church and in the world.

- ◆ Information overload—senses bombarded daily.

- ◆ Transient people in the church and in society.

- ◆ Global community mentality. (CNN has brought us all together.) We have the burdens of the world.

- ◆ Rapid and frequent changes in job market and economy.

- ◆ Radical changes in some congregations (division).

- ◆ Breakdown in home and family.

- ◆ Isolationist society (locked doors); no longer any sense of "neighborhood."

- ◆ Lack of leadership training for the future, as well as replacements now.

- ◆ Lack of motivation in followers to seek the lost (Luke 19:10).

- ◆ Lack of emphasis on biblical stewardship and giving.

- ◆ No modeling of evangelism and missions in the community.

- ◆ Failure to minister properly to the transgenerational society and congregation.

- ◆ A politically correct mentality in society, and even in the church.

- ◆ A failure to prioritize the kingdom properly (Matthew 6:33).

- ◆ Poor preaching and teaching in churches—not-learning churches.

- ◆ A continual breakdown in morality in the nation and in the church.

- ◆ Sheep without qualified shepherds (Acts 20:28).

- ◆ Deacons who aren't "deaconing."

Everywhere we look there are reminders and challenges as to why we need men to serve as faithful and productive deacons. The hour is late as we move toward the judgment (Hebrews 9:27). Even with all of us—elders, deacons, preachers, teachers, members—doing all we can, the task is becoming larger.

We need more servants! We need deacons who will accept the challenge and serve joyfully.

THE POWER OF JOY

It may surprise some to learn that joy is a major theme in the New Testament. And in the work of a servant, joy provides powerful motivation in accomplishing tasks for Christ. In the parable of the talents, Jesus spoke about the reward of joy for those who have served well: "Well done, good and faithful servant; you were faithful over a few things, I will make you ruler over many things. Enter into the joy of your lord" (Matthew 25:21). The same words are repeated in verse 23: "Enter into the joy of your lord." In contrast, the unprofitable servant received no joy: "And cast the unprofitable servant into the outer darkness. There will be weeping and gnashing of teeth" (Matthew 25:30). Do you feel joyful because you have used your talents wisely for the Lord? Are you serving joyfully as a deacon?

When you finish your assignment, do you feel a sense of joy?

Jesus sent the seventy out on a preaching and teaching mission (service mission). "Then the seventy returned with joy, saying, 'Lord, even the demons are subject to us in Your name'" (Luke 10:17). When you finish your assignment, do you feel a sense of joy?

When a servant does his work on earth, especially with regard to leading souls to the Lord, not only is there joy on earth, but there is joy in heaven. Jesus said, "I say to you that likewise there will be more joy in heaven over one sinner who repents than over ninety-nine just persons who need no repentance" (Luke 15:7). Do you create joy in heaven because of your serving in the gospel?

Joy was one of the things that characterized the church in the first century: "Therefore those who were scattered went everywhere preaching the word . . . There was great joy in that city" (Acts 8:4–8). When the conversion rate of the Gentiles was shared with the brethren in Jerusalem, it "caused great joy to all the brethren" (Acts 15:3). Is the congregation where you serve characterized by great joy?

In his listing of the fruit of the Spirit, the apostle Paul states that joy is one facet of the fruit: "But the fruit of the Spirit is love, joy, peace, longsuffering, kindness, goodness, faithfulness" (Galatians 5:22). Since the deacons that were chosen in Acts 6 were full of the Holy Spirit, we assume they were filled with joy. Is that fruit of the Spirit, joy, evident in your ministry and life as a deacon?

From the very beginning of the church, joy was one of the major attributes demonstrated by the members. "So continuing daily with one accord in the temple, and breaking bread from house to house, they ate their food with gladness and simplicity of heart" (Acts 2:46).

A servant in the Lord's church who serves out of a reluctant spirit is not pleasing God. Likewise, one who goes around with a frown on his face because he resents his assignment is not pleasing the one who has called him to serve. Read the book of Philippians and note how many times Paul refers to some form of joy. And keep in mind that he was a prisoner when he wrote that letter.

There is a dynamic power in joy. Note the following ten blessings of having a joyful heart:

→ BLESSINGS OF A JOYFUL HEART ←

◆ Joy has the power to create motivation.

◆ Joy has the power to create thanksgiving.

◆ Joy has the power to influence others.

◆ Joy has the power to maintain dedication.

◆ Joy has the power to produce excellence.

◆ Joy has the power to stimulate enthusiasm.

◆ Joy has the power to encourage the heart.

◆ Joy has the power to keep actions flowing.

◆ Joy has the power to finish a task.

◆ Joy has the power to attain a reward.

One of our theme songs should be: "I've got the joy, joy, joy, down in my heart. Where? Down in my heart to stay." It is a key to effective service as a deacon—any member, as for that matter—in the body of Christ.

BEWARE OF JOY ROBBERS

Since joy is one of the hallmarks of a Christian—especially one serving as a deacon in the Lord's church—we can be sure that Satan will do everything in his power to rob us of that joy. It reminds me of the eight-year-old who asked, "Daddy, are mules Christians?" In response, his father asked, "Son, why in the world would you ask such a silly question?" "Well, they have long faces too," replied the little boy. The old axiom is still true: "If you are happy, let your face and others know it." If you are serving the Lord out of the gladness of your heart, let others know it.

If Satan wanted to rob you of your joy in serving the Lord—and he does!—how would he do it? Here are a few things he would try.

⇝ SATAN'S MISSION ⇜

- Confuse your thoughts about how important your work in the church really is.

- Convince you that the assignment is busy-work, with no real value in advancing the kingdom.

- Help you to develop a "poor me" attitude. (That "nobody appreciates what I am doing" attitude is always a robber.)

- Prevent others from cooperating with you on a particular project. (You have to do it alone.)

- Prevent the leadership from issuing you authority to do the job. (That is a bucket of cold water on joy.)

- Drain your energy by wearing you down with unnecessary details.

- Cause you to dislike your assignment or to believe it has no value.

Joy Scale

On this scale, rate your present level of joy relative to your ministry assignment in the church:

No Joy 1 2 3 4 5 6 7 8 9 10 Full of Joy

Joy Improvement

We can all use a little more joy in our lives and ministries. Take a few moments and write a paragraph on how you can improve your joy in serving God:

_____

_____

_____

_____

_____

_____

_____

_____

_____

_____

_____

_____

_____

_____

_____

_____

_____

FOR THOUGHT AND DISCUSSION

1. What is your definition of joy?

2. What is the Bible's definition of joy?

3. Share some additional verses on joy.

4. Why should a deacon be joyful in his service to God?

5. What do we have to be joyful about as servants?

6. Discuss some ways Satan tries to rob us of joy?

7. What are some additional robbers of joy?

8. How does Psalm 118:24 relate to our study of joy?

9. What additional observations do you have?

10. How do you plan to use this lesson in your ministry?

✣ CASE STUDY ✦

The Park Street congregation's deacons were in a planning session trying to come up with an agenda for future study. Several subjects were suggested, but no one suggested a study of joy and its role in serving. How would you bring it up and try to sell it as a vital subject for deacons to study? Be specific and biblical in your approach.

Special Women Servants

WOMEN'S ROLES

Now let's look at 1 Timothy 3:11, "Likewise their wives must be reverent, not slanderers, temperate, faithful in all things." The role that women played in the Bible is given little consideration. In some congregations it is totally neglected.

Women servants! We have read about them and talked about them. We have seen them working in the church. But for some reason we have stayed away from taking an in-depth look at what God's word says about them. We have been diligent and quick to teach about the submission of women in the church and home but neglectful in teaching about their roles as servants in the church. If you want to raise eyebrows, just use the word *deaconess*.

Before we launch into this study, I must clarify that I do not personally believe a Christian woman has a right, or that she may receive permission to violate the following verses of Scripture which prohibit her from teaching or preaching in the assembly or usurping authority over men:

◆ 1 Timothy 2:11–12—"Let a woman learn in silence with all submission. And I do not permit a woman to teach or to have authority over a man, but to be in silence."

◆ 1 Corinthians 14:34–35—"Let your women keep silent in the churches, for they are not permitted to speak; but they are to be submissive, as the law also says. And if they want to learn something, let them ask their own husbands at home; for it is shameful for women to speak in church."

My goal in this lesson is to focus on what the Bible says about the role of women in serving God; to speak where the Bible speaks and be silent where the Bible is silent on this subject.

With these qualifiers I will share numerous biblical truths about how God has used women to do His work. Here are some of the Scriptures which exemplify the ministry (service) of women chosen by God.

WOMEN SERVANTS IN THE OLD TESTAMENT

Why look at women who served in the Old Testament? Here is Paul's answer: "For whatever things were written before were written for our learning, that we through the patience and comfort of the Scriptures might have hope" (Romans 15:4). Concerning the value of an Old Testament example, Paul also wrote: "Now all these things happened to them as examples, and they were written for our admonition, upon whom the ends of the ages have come" (1 Corinthians 10:11).

◆ *Sarah* was a servant of God. That conclusion is deduced from her activities and experiences with Abraham in Genesis 12–18. She not only left her security at home to go with her husband to a strange land to serve God, but she was also chosen by God to be the mother of a great nation.

◆ *Miriam* was a servant of God. "Then Miriam the prophetess, the sister of Aaron, took the timbrel in her hand; and all the women went out after her with timbrels and with dances. And Miriam answered them: 'Sing to the Lord, for He has triumphed gloriously! The horse and its rider He has thrown into the sea!'" (Exodus 15:20–21). She was chosen by God to lead a victory celebration after Israel had successfully crossed the Red Sea.

◆ *Rahab* was a servant of God. In Joshua 2 we read how she was used by God to hide the Hebrew spies and provide a means of their escape. She was honored by God in that she was spared when the city was destroyed. She was also honored to be among the ancestors of Jesus Christ (Matthew 1:5). Read Joshua 2 to see what this woman did in her service to God and His people.

◆ *Deborah* was a servant of God. She was chosen by God to be the fourth judge in Israel. "Now Deborah, a prophetess, the wife of Lapidoth, was judging Israel at that time. And she would sit under the palm tree of Deborah between Ramah and Bethel in mountains of Ephraim. And the children of Israel came up to her for judgment" (Judges 4:4–5). She commanded Barak in his efforts of war (Judges 4:14–24). After the victory we read: "Then Deborah and Barak the son of Abinoam sang on that day, saying: 'When leaders lead in Israel, when the people willingly offer themselves, bless the Lord'" (Judges 5:1–2). God chose a woman to be a leader in Israel!

◆ *Ruth* was a servant of God. Ruth was chosen by God to be a vital link to David and the royal house of Judah. Through her, a connection developed between Israel and Moab. Ruth worked in the fields and gained favor with those in authority. Ruth married Boaz but she remained faithful to her mother-in-law, Naomi. There is little doubt in the mind of one reading Ruth that she was not only a servant of man, but also, and more important, a servant of God. Read the book of Ruth for more details.

◆ *Hannah* was a servant of God. When we meet her in 1 Samuel 1, she is beseeching God for a child. Eli comes on the scene and doesn't understand what's going on. He accuses her of being drunk or in league with Belial (1 Samuel 1:13–16). She assures him that she is not. Rather, she wants a child who will glorify God. God blesses her with a son, Samuel (1:20–21), whom she dedicated to the service of the Lord (1:24–28). God later called Samuel to a dynamic ministry within Israel (3:1–19). Again we see God used a woman to fulfill a great purpose among His people.

> *Ruth was not only a servant of man, she was a servant of God.*

◆ *Esther* was a servant of God. This woman, whose name literally means "a star," was an orphan in Israel and became the wife (and queen) of Ahasuerus, the king of Persia. She had been raised by her cousin Mordecai, who held a position of low rank in the royal palace. God's people were threatened with destruction, and Esther rose, with God's help, to be their deliverer. In the midst of the crisis, Mordecai encouraged Esther with these words: "Yet who knows whether you have come to the kingdom for such a time as this?" (Esther 4:14). We now know the answer was yes; she was right in the middle of God's timing as His servant.

There are other women servants in the Old Testament, but these seven are adequate examples of how God used women to fulfill His mission among His people. They were preserved in the Bible for our learning: God uses women! Women have a place in God's service.

Women Servants in the New Testament

For many readers of this book, some of the women mentioned in the New Testament will be more meaningful, because they are not presented in the Old Testament. Here is a list of some New Testament women who served God, and in most cases, the church too.

- ◆ *Elizabeth* was a servant of God. This lady was the wife of Zacharias and was chosen by God to be the mother of John the Baptist, the man who would be the forerunner of the Messiah (Luke 1:5–80). She was the cousin of Mary, the mother of Jesus (Luke 1:36). She was used by the Holy Spirit to encourage Mary (Luke 1:41–45).

- ◆ *Mary* was a servant of God. Most would agree that when God chose her womb through which Jesus would be born, she was elevated to the highest honor any woman could be afforded; not to be worshiped as some do, but just as a reminder that God doesn't view women as inferior or useless. Every student of the Bible knows the account of the virgin birth of Jesus (Luke 1:26–45; 2:1–7). Notice the words of Mary: "My soul magnifies the Lord, and my spirit has rejoiced in God my Savior. For he has regarded the lowly state of his maidservant; for, behold, henceforth all generations will call me blessed" (Luke 1:46–48).

- ◆ *Mary and Martha* were servants of God. Here's Luke's account of an occasion when these sisters had a problem over serving:

  > Now it happened as they went that He entered a certain village; and a certain woman named Martha welcomed Him into her house. And she had a sister called Mary, who also sat at Jesus' feet and heard His word. But Martha was distracted with much serving, and she approached Him and said,

"Lord, do You not care that my sister has left me to serve alone? Therefore tell her to help me." And Jesus answered and said to her, "Martha, Martha, you are worried and troubled about many things. But one thing is needed, and Mary has chosen that good part, which will not be taken away from her" (Luke 10:38–42).

◆ *Mary Magdalene* was a servant of God. Mary was chosen by God to be the first at the empty tomb from which Jesus had been resurrected (John 20:1). She was the first to announce the resurrection to Peter (John 20:2–9). Jesus appeared first to her after His resurrection (John 20:14–17). "Mary Magdalene came and told the disciples that she had seen the Lord, and that He had spoken these things to her" (John 20:18). I find it very significant that Jesus chose a woman, Mary Magdalene, to show Himself alive from the dead, the very event that proved without a shadow of a doubt that He was the Messiah (Romans 1:4). Jesus respected women; He used them in God's service.

◆ *Philip* had four daughters who served God. When Peter preached his sermon on the Day of Pentecost, he quoted from Joel's prophecy (Joel 2:28–30) these words: "But this is what was spoken by the prophet Joel: 'And it shall come to pass in the last days, says God, that I will pour out of My Spirit on all flesh; your sons and your daughters shall prophesy, your young men shall see visions, your old men shall dream dreams'" (Acts 2:16–17). Later, after the establishment of the church, we read this account: "On the next day we . . . entered the house of Philip the evangelist, who was one of the seven; and stayed with him. Now this man had four virgin daughters who prophesied" (Acts 21:8–9). We are not given any more information about these women. I assume, however, that they did not teach "over men" or in the assembly. But someway, somehow, God used them to teach.

◆ *Priscilla* was a servant of God. She was the wife of Aquila, and together she and Aquila were an evangelistic team, having first met Paul in Corinth (Acts 18:1–2). Paul gave that great missionary couple this accolade: "Greet Priscilla and Aquila, my fellow workers in Christ Jesus, who risked their own necks for my life, to whom not only I give thanks, but also all the churches of the Gentiles. Likewise greet the church that is in their house" (Romans 16:3–5; cf. 1 Corinthians 16:19). In Acts

18:24–28 we learn that Pricilla helped her husband teach Apollos: "So he began to speak boldly in the synagogue. When Aquila and Priscilla heard him, they took him aside and explained to him the way of God more accurately" (Acts 18:26). The Greek language in this verse makes it clear that both were involved in teaching Apollos.

♦ *Lydia* was a servant of God. Lydia was a successful business woman who worshiped God. "Now a certain woman named Lydia heard us. She was a seller of purple from the city of Thyatira, who worshiped God. The Lord opened her heart to heed the things spoken by Paul. And when she and her household were baptized, she begged us, saying, 'If you have judged me to be faithful to the Lord, come to my house and stay.' So she persuaded us" (Acts 16:14–15). Lydia was a hospitable servant. When Paul and Silas were released from prison they went to her house (Acts 16:40).

♦ *Chloe* was a servant of God. It seems evident that her house played a vital role in distributing information among believers. Paul said, "For it has been declared to me concerning you, my brethren, by those of Chloe's household, that there are contentions among you" (1 Corinthians 1:11). We know nothing else about this woman mentioned by Paul.

♦ *Euodias and Syntyche* were servants of God. Paul wrote: "I implore Euodia and I implore Syntyche to be of the same mind in the Lord. And I urge you also, true companion, help these women who labored with me in the gospel, with Clement also, and the rest of my fellow workers, whose names are in the Book of Life" (Philippians 4:2–3). Some think these two women were having a "Mary and Martha" problem over serving; the text isn't clear. One thing is clear; Paul had women serving with him in the gospel.

♦ *Older women* are to be servants of God. While Paul doesn't give names, he does give instructions in regard to the responsibility of older women to teach younger women. "The older women likewise, that they be reverent in behavior, not slanderers, not given to much wine, teachers of good things—that they admonish the young women to love their husbands, to love their children, to be discreet, chaste, homemakers, good, obedient to their own husbands, that the word of God may not be blasphemed"

(Titus 2:3–5). What a need in all congregations! Women serving as teachers; the older instructing the younger.

◆ *Phoebe* was a servant of God. When Paul begins to commend various workers in the gospel, he says this about Phoebe, whom he lists first: "I commend to you Phoebe our sister, who is a servant *[diakonas]* of the church in Cenchrea, that you may receive her in the Lord in a manner worthy of the saints, and assist her in whatever business she has need of you; for indeed she has been a helper of many and of myself also" (Romans 16:1–2).

◆ *Phoebe* is described as a servant of the church *(ousan diakonon tēs ekklēsias)*. We have noted the meaning of *deacon* numerous times in our study. In this verse there is no reason to deduce more than Paul is saying: Phoebe, a woman servant, served the church, as Paul did. There is no indication here or elsewhere in the New Testament that there was an official office of deaconesses. Secular writings, such as the *Apostolic Constitutions,* contain numerous allusions to deaconesses. It seems within biblical authority to appoint women over services within the bounds set by Scripture.

From these biblical examples, it is clear that God used many women to serve Him and His people, and the same is true today. We need women servants in the church, women who are qualified to do special works of ministry as described in the Bible.

A LOOK AT A SPECIAL TEXT

Consider one additional portion of Scripture before we close this chapter: "Likewise their wives must be reverent, not slanderers, temperate, faithful in all things" (1 Timothy 3:11). Looking closely at the verse in the English text we note that "women must" ("their wives must" KJV) is in italics, which means it has been added by the translators. It is not in the Greek text. Leaving "their wives must" out, we have this reading: "Likewise, wives reverent, not slanderers, temperate, faithful in all things." It is not clear in the original text if the wives of deacons are under consideration or wives in general who serve the church. The Greek word translated "wives" is *gunaikas* and may also be translated "women."

In his commentary on 1 and 2 Timothy and Titus, Dr. Denny Petrillo offers this observation:

> Wives of deacons—This is again ambiguous. There is nothing in the Greek text (such as a possessive) that would indicate these women were connected with the deacons by marriage. The Greek indicates that these women are a group by themselves. Guy N. Woods correctly notes: "Were wives of deacons intended, it is likely that the apostle would have followed usual New Testament practice of referring to them as 'your wives.'" (Quality Publications, Abilene, Texas, 1998), 44.

QUALIFICATIONS OF WOMEN SERVANTS

In this verse there are several "must be" qualifications set forth for women servants, regardless of whether Paul is speaking to wives or women in general. Women assigned to special ministries must meet these requirements:

⇢ QUALIFICATIONS FOR WOMEN SERVANTS ⇠

◆ *Reverent.* This is the same word *(semnos)* used in 1 Timothy 3:4–8, and refers to the dignity, nobleness, and seriousness with which the woman servant conducts herself. She is a godly woman, serving God in holiness (1 Timothy 2:9–15). Paul stresses that elders, deacons, and women servants must possess a sound and serious approach to serving God and the church.

◆ *Not slanderers.* Women servants must not be malicious gossips. They must not use speech to harm the reputation and effectiveness of others. They are to be "swift to hear, slow to speak" (James 1:19), and must be "speaking the truth in love" (Ephesians 4:15).

◆ *Temperate.* These women servants are temperate and self-controlled. The same word is used in 1 Timothy 3:2 and in Titus 2:2, and also denotes being vigilant in what is being pursued. They have a singleness of mind and purpose in their service to the Lord and the church.

◆ *Faithful in all things.* These special women servants are trustworthy. They may be trusted to start, continue, and finish a task in an honorable way. A congregation that doesn't have elders, deacons, and women servants faithfully fulfilling their duties will be in disarray. All servants must be faithful in all things (1 Corinthians 4:2; Revelation 2:10).

SUMMARY OBSERVATIONS

Let's take a few minutes and summarize what we have learned in this chapter about women servants in the Bible.

1. It is clear that God used women in His work in both the Old and New Testament.

2. Their service ranged from being political leaders to waiting on tables.

3. They were teachers of the gospel.

4. They were part of ministry teams.

5. They served church leaders.

6. They were singled out for recognition.

7. They had a special responsibility to other women.

8. They were not to go beyond the boundaries set by God's word.

9. They were courageous.

10. They made major contributions to the growth and stability of the church.

11. In some cases where special ministries were involved, they must have met certain qualifications.

While the obvious thrust of this book has been the deacons in the Lord's church, it seemed appropriate to me to include this lesson on the place and role of women servants in the church. In my experience, Christian women have been responsible for some dynamic contributions. They are part of God's mighty force. May we take their work seriously and provide education and training for these great servants in the church.

FOR THOUGHT AND DISCUSSION

1. Why are some church members afraid of the word *deaconess?*

   _____

2. Why has the church been reluctant to recognize the role of women in service?

   _____

3. What restrictions has God placed on woman's service? Why?

   _____

   _____

4. Discuss the account of Mary and Martha serving Jesus. What were the issues? Why?

   _____

   _____

5. How did Priscilla and Aquila work together as an evangelistic couple?

   _____

6. How are the older women in your congregation teaching and leading the younger women?

   _____

7. Discuss the role and place of Phoebe in Paul's ministry?

   _____

8. Discuss some of the ministries women may be assigned.

   _____

9. How can the church encourage more women to become involved in serving?

   _____

10. What additional observations do you have?

    _____

→ **CASE STUDY** ←

The Lee Street congregation needed someone to supervise the elementary Bible class department, K–6. When an elder brought up the name of a sister, an elementary school principal, several protested, saying the position was not within the bounds of a woman's work in the church. What would your position have been in this situation? Be biblical and specific in your answer.

_____

_____

_____

_____

_____

_____

_____

_____

_____

_____

_____

_____

_____

_____

_____

_____

_____

_____

_____

_____

_____